THE

# EMOTIONAL
# INTELLIGENCE

ADVANTAGE

# THE
# EMOTIONAL
# INTELLIGENCE
## ADVANTAGE

## MASTERING CHANGE AND
## DIFFICULT CONVERSATIONS

# AMY JACOBSON

WILEY

First published 2025 by John Wiley & Sons Australia, Ltd

© John Wiley & Sons Australia, Ltd 2025

The right of Amy Jacobson to be identified as the author of *The Emotional Intelligence Advantage* has been asserted in accordance with law.

ISBN: 978-1-394-33794-1

A catalogue record for this book is available from the National Library of Australia

*Registered Office*
John Wiley & Sons Australia, Ltd. Level 4, 600 Bourke Street, Melbourne, VIC 3000, Australia

For details of our global editorial offices, customer services, and more information about Wiley products visit us at www.wiley.com.

Wiley also publishes its books in a variety of electronic formats and by print-on-demand. Some content that appears in standard print versions of this book may not be available in other formats.

Cover design by Wiley
Cover image: © orsonsurf/Getty Images

Set in 11.5/14.5pt Warnock Pro by Straive, Chennai, India.

Printed in Singapore
M134672_090425

# CONTENTS

# ABOUT THE AUTHOR

Amy is an emotional intelligence (EI) specialist who challenges and disrupts people's mindsets to own it, take control and be unstoppable.

With her fascination for the human mind, neuroscience and neurolinguistic programming (NLP), Amy balances tough love and infectious energy to create purpose-driven teams who *get results*!

Amy takes people out of their comfort zone with her methodology, challenging their mindset and helping them bring ownership and purpose to every work day.

Amy is driven to break through the misconception of EI and see people reach their full potential, embrace their strengths and be great human beings.

Based in Perth, Australia, with an international reach, Amy is a media personality across TV, radio and print. She delivers keynotes, EI programs, workshops and coaching across the world in all industries and sectors.

As a wife to her supportive husband and best friend Mark, mother to two amazing children, Amelia and Koen, and business owner of Amy Jacobson Pty Ltd, Amy completely gets the challenge of balancing all the roles in our life while still finding time to include herself somewhere near the top of the list.

Amy defines success as being happy. 'Find the things that make you happy and spend as much time as you can doing them. It really is that simple.' Travelling and enjoying adventures with her beautiful family brings Amy happiness, along with seeing people's faces light up as they 'find' themselves.

# ACKNOWLEDGEMENTS

The motivation to write this book came from a client requesting a summary of one of my emotional intelligence workshops, specifically the emotional intelligence process. While aspects of this workshop were detailed in my first book, *Emotional Intelligence: A simple and actionable guide to increasing performance, engagement and ownership*, the parts they really wanted were new additions. In my head I thought, 'If I'm going to write a summary, I might as well write another book …' And voilà! Here we are ☺.

So, my first thank you goes to my client for the small, unintentional request that turned into this book!

My family thought it a bit extreme to write another book rather than a summary, but they are used to my shenanigans so, like absolute champions, they supported me like they always do and celebrated all the milestones. I have so much love for my family, my friends who have become family and the support networks in my life. There really is nothing more important to me.

The year 2024 was big for work travel, so a large chunk of this book was written on planes. Thank you to the wifi in the air, the people who had to sit next to me tap, tap, tapping away, and the endless supply of snacks that got me through words, pages and time zones. (By the way, this book goes really well with chocolate of any type, so treat yourself!)

I'm ridiculously grateful for the opportunity to do what I do. I really do work with the most interesting and fantastic people around the world and get to learn so much from them in return.

It still absolutely makes my day to hear from people who have read my first book, attended my programs or heard me through media, in particular when they tell me the learnings really hit home and made a difference to who they are today and to their relationships.

Sending love and thanks to you all, far and wide. Xx

# PROLOGUE

Traditional workplace and leadership expectations have changed. I'm not talking small changes; I'm talking massive shifts. Massive shifts in mindset, in focus, in expectations and in priorities.

Emotional intelligence (or EI) has become a necessity in workplaces and the commitment to people's wellbeing now sits at the top of many organisations' agendas.

The unexpected and unprecedented changes that we have faced, and continue to face, in the workplace have provided a new lens and have us looking at the work component of our lives in a completely different way.

## Ask

Do we live to work, or do we work to live? Or is there a middle ground? What is our true purpose in life and is our

(continued)

definition of how we define 'success' realistic and not just materialistic? So many unanswered questions lurk in our minds, taking up real estate space and making us rethink our relationship with work.

# The current state of the workplace

Workplaces have been turned on their heads as they watch their employees go through these changes, reacting in slightly different ways. Some cope better than others; some really struggle. We tend to take for granted the impact that people have on our bottom line, products/services and the customer. But we are quickly reminded that without our people being able to work physically and mentally, there is no workplace. The bottom line, the products/services and the customer become totally irrelevant without the people!

This shift has been evident across the world as we watch people prioritise what is important in life, and for many, it isn't spending endless long hours working.

Resources seem to have become low across every industry as people decide to reduce their hours, switch to something they like or enjoy doing and find the ultimate life balance. It creates confusion and leaves us wondering how we can suddenly be so short staffed or under resourced across every industry even if our workload and head count hasn't changed. But it isn't the number of resources or our workload that are necessarily changing; it is our relationship with work and what we are willing to give that are changing. How many hours and how much focus are people now willing to dedicate to work? For many people, this number has decreased dramatically.

It had become such standard and accepted practice in the past that we work 10- to 12-hour days and sometimes without any breaks. While this is not always quality work or healthy for us, it's what many of us did and had accepted as the norm of work. In some instances, being forced to take downtime and spend more time at home increased the value of life outside of work, reminding us how it felt to let go of some of that stress and refocus on the parts of our life that are important. Once people start to get a taste of it, they want more of this balance and more time to focus on the important things. With this we see decreased working hours and some people simply reverting to the standard hours of seven- to eight-hour days. The fact that we built our workforce requirements on people working much longer hours than they were being paid or contracted to do, is our downfall.

For some industries, downtime wasn't an option, and the changes and intensity are increasing due to resource shortages or increased needs from the community. Those 10- to 12-hour days are becoming even longer and it feels like the impossible is upon us without any sign of relief in the near future. This is like the straw that broke the camel's back and for some people, it is enough to quit their job, their industry and their relentless dedication to work. Some people just aren't willing to give this much of themselves to work any longer. They don't want the stress or the responsibilities.

There is a definite shift in personal priorities. People are more comfortable in themselves, and we are encouraging each other to be real, to feel and speak up in the workplace like anywhere else in our lives. It's not just 'do what I say and not what I do'. It's 'speak up and talk about how you are feeling and the role that work plays in your life'.

Employees have so much more choice. A new job opportunity is around almost every corner now. Expectations are changing and increasing as new generations enter the workforce. The hierarchical difference between the managers and employees is decreasing and the confidence and rights of employees are increasing. Whether this is right or wrong is irrelevant. We are not here to argue what the workplace should look like; we are here to accept that this is what it does look like and as leaders, we must adapt and lead the way.

Leaders have leveraged their known and lived leadership skills to support their team members as much as possible with an increased focus on people leadership. For some team members, this is enough, while for the majority of others it isn't. Leadership is being redefined and a leader without the ability to leverage and build their emotional intelligence finds it very difficult to manage the variety of people, the shifting demands and the different responses to situations.

## Ask

Why do these changes impact people differently? Why are the needs and expectations of people so varied?

Leadership never was a blueprint or a template, yet it's becoming even more ad hoc with the need to adapt to every situation and person. As we continue to bring more humanistic approaches into the workforce and encourage people to be authentic and real, the variance will continue to grow. The upside is that performance, engagement and creativity also grow by giving people more ownership and freedom to think. However, they also break the 'cookie mould' approach and we end up with big variations in personalities, attitudes, expectations and emotional responses.

Basic leadership skills are no longer enough. It is going to take every ounce of our emotional intelligence to first understand ourselves, then understand what each of the people around us is going through and how they are wired or what makes them 'tick', before we can even consider what they need from us as leaders. It's challenging even the greatest and most experienced leaders as they take a step back and focus on the fundamental basics of understanding and adapting to the person in front of them. We can reap the benefits of having modern and humanistic workplaces, but not without addressing the new challenges arising from the change.

Difficult conversations are becoming more prevalent due to the changes and level of human interaction. I don't think I've ever met anyone who loves to have a difficult conversation. I'd even say it would have to be one of the most avoided things we do as leaders, resulting in the situation snowballing while we look the other way hoping it will go away. When we do have the difficult conversations, they are poorly executed, lack outcomes and become a defensive battle between the people involved.

This is attracting attention and becoming a priority for managing directors, chief executive officers (CEOs) and pretty much everyone at the high-level running of an organisation that relies on people to achieve results. They recognise that the bottom line and profit, the products and services, and their customers are irrelevant if they haven't got their people right. They want help with the people in their organisation, but also, they want help for themselves and their own leadership skills to lead the team from the top in an environment overflowing with change in priorities, change in operations and change in people when emotions run wild.

This is why the need for EI and the role it plays is now much more present and really is a necessity for all workplaces.

## What is emotional intelligence?

Whenever there are human beings involved in any situation, there are also emotions. Every second of every day we are feeling some kind of emotion. Emotional intelligence (EI) is our ability to recognise these emotions, manage the emotions as they play out, and understand the impact they have on the people around us and the outcome of the situation.

From a world-renowned expert in EI, Dr Travis Bradberry's research shows that only 36 per cent of people can accurately identify emotions as they occur. This helps to explain why EI can be a challenging skill to master.

Some people are lucky enough to be born with the natural skill to identify and manage their emotions, but the millions of other people need to learn and work on growing their EI.

EI can be taught. I've taught many people in this field. The key is you must *want* to learn it. In a workplace with extensive human interaction, it is a 'must' to not only have the awareness of our emotions as they occur, but to also have the skills that are required to manage, process and align the emotions.

# EI is not about what we know or what we can do; it's the how and why we do it!

The 'what we know or what we can do' is our IQ. This is our knowledge, education, talent and what we can deliver. The 'how and why we do it' is our EI. How well we interact with others, how we make people feel, how we manage emotions, the effectiveness of our communication and the purpose or 'why' behind what we do.

Neither is more important than the other. Our IQ will only take us so far in life before we require our EI to kick in. Equally, our EI will only take us so far in life before our IQ needs to kick in. I like to say that often it's our IQ that gets us the job, but it's our EI that gets us promoted! Bradberry's studies also show that 90 per cent of top performers are also high in EI, whereas only 20 per cent of bottom performers are high in EI. So it's the balance of both EI and IQ that we are striving for to become a high performer.

There are five key concepts around EI: Own It, Face It, Feel It, Ask It and Drive It. These concepts build the foundational skills of EI. I truly believe there is no such thing as an emotionally intelligent person. I teach EI and I would never refer to myself as being emotionally intelligent. Each and every one of us has emotional intelligence within us and we have a choice in every situation. Do we respond in an emotionally intelligent way or do we not? Sometimes we get it right and sometimes we really don't. My teenage daughter calls me out on this at times saying, 'That wasn't very emotionally intelligent, was it, Mum?' And she is absolutely right. Sometimes my emotional brain takes over and I don't get it right first go. It's what we choose to do when we don't get it right the first time that really shows our level of emotional intelligence. Do we have the awareness to Own It, get our emotions under control, understand the impact we've had on others, apologise when appropriate and have another go to constantly develop our EI? It's not about perfection every time; it starts with self-awareness and is something we work on every day.

In my book, *Emotional Intelligence: A simple and actionable guide to increasing performance, engagement and ownership*, I dug deep into each of the five EI key concepts. I wrote about what each of these concepts means and how to build our core skills in all five areas to grow and respond in a more emotionally intelligent way.

The five key concepts are:

1.   Own It
2.   Face It
3.   Feel It
4.   Ask It
5.   Drive

In chapter 1 I'll delve more deeply into these.

## What to expect from this book

This book applies the core concepts of EI at the next level. I will show you how to take the practical side of the concepts and put them into action every day to be a better leader and a better human being. It's no longer about knowing what EI is and the best ways to use it; it's about taking action and applying EI in some of the most challenging situations that occur in the workplace.

You'll see that the book is divided into four parts:

- *Part I: The emotional intelligence process*

  In part I I'll show you how to understand and follow the emotional intelligence process, not just the concept. You will learn how to recognise where people are in their own emotional intelligence process and what support they will need from you to help them move through each step of the process effectively in readiness for starting the process again as the situation shifts.

  I'll help you identify how this process occurs constantly in everything you do and the role it plays in causing conflict, confrontations and denial — as well as lack of progress in individuals, teams and organisations. It is not just a one-time process but a fluent and continuous process relying on your EI every step of the way.

- *Part II: Change intelligence*

  In part II we will move away from process-driven change management. It's often not the change that isn't effective: it's the lack of buy-in from the people that causes the problems. You will come to understand what actually happens in our mind as it transitions with change and the huge role that the emotional intelligence process plays within change. Ticking a box for each step of the change management plan is not enough. Change involves developing new neural pathways in our mind, and this requires creating new habits and beliefs — but, more importantly, knowing how to let go of the old ones first.

We don't have to love change — in fact, we need people who love consistency in every workplace — but we do need to accept change and transition our mind with the change. If we skip the mind transition, we end up with people still holding onto change that happened years ago.

- *Part III: Difficult conversations*

  This is where we will address what is easily the most avoided part of leadership — even possibly the most avoided part of life! You'll learn how to not overthink difficult conversations, overanalyse them, become a robot in defence mode and blow it all out of proportion.

  I'll show you how to implement a core framework that will bring a humanistic and honest approach to the difficult conversation to ensure it is an effective conversation and that the desired outcomes are achieved for everyone. And it won't just be a one-off followed by a relapse, but a way to create positive change and ownership through emotions.

  Difficult conversations don't always take place top-down. Some of the most difficult conversations happen when we are communicating with people in positions above us or equal to us. When we have the right skills and approach, and we follow the emotional response, magic happens.

- *Part IV: High-performing teams*

  Behind every high-performing team you will find alignment, trust and great communication. I'll show you how you can complement your newfound communication skills with the elements of an aligned team led by a great leader who knows how to balance their time across strategic, operational and people leadership to get the team on the same page with a common purpose.

I will discuss how to create trust, which is one of the foundations of a high-performing workplace environment, and how to ensure each person feels safe and part of a culturally unified workplace.

We will break down the word 'trust' and its drivers to understand how trust is created and developed, and what it takes to create a high-performing team where people can trust each other and the space they play in.

So that's the crux of the book: using the five key concepts as a framework, we will take your EI to the next level and learn how to apply it in the most common workplace challenges.

It's time to step up our game. Are you ready for the ride?

Part I

# THE EMOTIONAL INTELLIGENCE PROCESS

Life is not static. Nor is our mind.

Learning information and new skills will always be a moving and growing process. Even the application of the learnings become part of a process as they form with our existing habits and day-to-day workings.

Our mind goes through processes based on the neural pathways that run through it. These pathways are created based on our values, beliefs, habits, experiences and memories. At the start of each pathway is a trigger (something that occurs) and the pathway leads through a number of consecutive steps, arriving at an emotional feeling and response. So, when *this* happens, I respond like *this*. Millions of these pathways exist within our mind, detailing processes for different situations.

Whether it is our morning routine, a simple 'bless you' that follows a sneeze or hugging someone when they are upset, processes drive what we do and help us to get from the start of an occurrence to the outcome that we desire. It is the process that each one of us takes that determines our level of comfort and acceptance of what is happening and our ability to move forward.

EI also forms a process. After years of studying people in this field, I have found that there is a process that occurs within our mind through our emotions when situations happen all the way through to our response and acceptance. Like any process, having an understanding of the steps of this process, which step a person is at and how to support them to move through the process provides a far superior outcome than being left wondering and confused as to why they are reacting the way they are.

In part I, I will teach you the EI process, how to recognise it in every situation and how to master the ability to support people through the process, resulting in the outcome we desire, with everyone in acceptance and ready to move forward.

# Chapter 1

# UNDERSTANDING THE EI PROCESS

Using the five key concepts of EI as a foundation, let's look at how the EI process works and each of the steps our mind goes through.

The five key concepts of EI are not stand-alone concepts. They are an ever-moving fluent process, from step 1 through to step 5. These are detailed in figure 1.1 (overleaf).

This process is evident in every part of our lives. In fact, you are going through it right now as you read this book. You will also be going through the process in every other part of your life simultaneously. Everyone in your workplace is also going through it at their own speed — each at different steps and dealing with the steps in different ways. Regardless of who you are, every human being goes through this process regularly.

**1** **Own It**
Owning the reality of the situation and being aware of what we can and can't control. Whether we like it or not, this is happening and we must Own It!

**2** **Face It**
Face all the emotions that are occurring due to the situation. Recognise the emotion, understand where it is coming from, Face It and process the emotion.

**3** **Feel It**
Feel the impact the people around us are experiencing. We are out of our own heads; it's not about us. Now it's about the people around us and how they are feeling.

**4** **Ask It**
Ask the logical questions to understand the what, when and how. Answer all questions that other people ask us with context and meaning.

**5** **Drive It**
Drive whatever it takes to move the situation and solution through to the next step. This is the action step. The doing step. Drive It is when we make it happen.

**Figure 1.1:** the five-step EI process

How well we leverage our EI will determine whether we move onto the next step or get stuck looping, not knowing how to move forward.

**It is our effectiveness throughout the EI process that influences performance, relationships and our results in any workplace or situation.**

Let's walk through the steps to understand how the EI process works.

# 1. Own It

Own It is our self-awareness, and acceptance of the reality of the situation. It's taking responsibility for who we are and why we do what we do, as well as understanding the way in which we are wired. EI is not necessarily about changing who we are: it's understanding the wirings within our brain and working with them rather than against them. Yes, there is always the opportunity to grow and develop, but you also need to be true to yourself and remain authentic based on your values and beliefs.

To begin the process, it's best to picture yourself standing in the void before Own It — in other words, you are yet to own it: the process hasn't started as yet.

**If I could sum up EI in two words, it really would be Own It.**

What I mean by this is:

- Own who you are.
- Own the decisions you have made in your life that have brought you to where you are today.
- Own the values and beliefs that are driving those decisions.
- Own how well you manage your own emotions in every situation.
- Own the impact you have on the people around you.

- Own how well you communicate.
- Own what you have achieved to date in your life because everything you have achieved so far in life is on you, so Own It!

We become self-aware of the role we play in the situation and the purpose of our role. Not only is it our self-awareness but it's also acceptance of the reality of the current situation. There are some situations that we have (or had) very little control or influence over. We might have originally had influence and input but now that the final decision has been made, this is it. It might not be what we wanted, or thought was best, but the decision has been made and now it is reality. It could be driven by the environment, like an outbreak or a pandemic, a political decision or a situation that is far greater than our reach over which we have no control. We simply must accept that this is happening, weigh up the choices available to us and accept reality. It is happening whether we like it or not.

Here are some examples of Own It as step 1 of the EI process:

- *System changes:* Altering an existing user system, platform or process in the workplace is a common and ongoing part of work. They are not always wanted or welcomed. Sometimes there is very little notice or engagement. But once the decision has been made that the system changes are occurring, we have got to own this fact. Own it and accept it.
- *A new job:* There are so many factors that could lead to getting a new job: a choice we have made, a redundancy or termination, a relocation or another reason why we believe we need to change jobs.

To move forward, we must own the reality that we are changing jobs. This is happening. We are committed and it's no longer a 'need' or 'want': it is a 'do'. We are doing this. We are getting a new job!

- *Reading this book:* At some point you must have heard of or seen this book and decided to read it. You couldn't be reading this line right now unless you owned the fact that you are committing to read it right now. Whether that's making the time or creating the environment or whatever it took you to get to this point where you are reading these lines, you had to Own It to do it.

To Own It, stay who you are, accept reality and become a better version of you!

## Ask

What is happening in your life that you are struggling to accept the reality of? How well do you Own It? Do you understand what makes you 'tick'? What wirings are driving who you are? Are you able to accept reality and work with what is happening rather than wishing it wasn't? What is one thing that you can own today to continue to move forward?

# 2. Face It

This is where self-regulation and management of our emotions occurs. The key concept of Face It aligns with our ability to face all our emotions, process them and get them under control. We can't ignore them because they will find a way to impact our lives and force us to face them at some point.

When we look at this concept as step 2 of the process, this is where our emotional brain kicks in and can rapidly bounce us from one emotion to the next in relation to how we are feeling about a situation. These emotions stem from our amygdala, which is a small, almond-shaped part of our brain that processes our emotions. The amygdala is often referred to as our 'emotional brain' whereas our neo cortex is often referred to as our logical brain. The neo cortex is a large part of our brain where most of the analysis related to reasoning, perception, cognition and movement occurs. Both the logical and emotional brain play an important role in our day-to-day living. The standard process is that the logical brain receives information first and acts based on its analysis of the information before the emotional brain kicks in. However, this doesn't always happen. Sometimes an emotional hijack occurs, which means that instead of the information going to our logical brain first to be analysed and understood it goes to our emotional brain first and we respond emotionally before our logical brain has been engaged. Therefore, it is overwritten with emotion and very little logic.

These emotions are completely created and driven by us.

No-one can make us feel angry; no-one can make us feel happy or sad or scared or any of the many emotions we feel. As much as we like to pass the buck and make it someone else's fault that we feel this way, it really isn't the case. How we choose to feel and respond in every situation is one of the only things we have control over in life.

This feeling and response is guided by the neural pathways in our mind. We have 86 to 100 billion neurons floating around in our heads and when these neurons touch or connect with each other, it is called neuroplasticity. Neuroplasticity forms our neural pathways. At the start of each neural pathway is a trigger, as in a situation or occurrence, and at the end of the pathway lies the emotional response. So, when 'this' happens (trigger activated and we follow the neural pathway in our mind), we feel like 'this' (emotional response embedded at the end of the pathway).

These pathways have been created from birth and will continue throughout our lives based on our experiences, values, beliefs and long-term memory. Some of us will have similar neural pathways because we have had similar upbringings, environments and aligned values and beliefs, meaning we may respond in similar ways with similar emotions, but it is still not the situation or person causing the response — it's our embedded neural pathways that are similar and leading us to the outcome. You can imagine how these pathways would differ across people, workplaces, cultures, countries and the world with different values and beliefs.

The situation or person happens and one of our neural pathways is triggered, leading us to choose the emotional response that sits at the end of that pathway based on our long-term memory, experiences, values and beliefs. *We* created these pathways so *we* have control and can change these pathways throughout our life. Is it easy? No. Is it possible? Yes. It's all about choice.

**These first two key EI concepts — Own It and Face It — are in our head; they are 100 per cent about us.**

Without owning and facing it, we can't move forward and will find ourselves looping back and forth in our own head between Own It and Face It, making no real progress yet exasperating our emotions.

Face It can at times be interchanged with Own It and we may need to face these emotions before we can even own the reality. So, it might mean we start at step 2 by facing our emotions first, then move on to owning the reality after we have processed the emotions. Or we might have already owned the reality but when we go to face the emotions, we struggle to process them and move through our emotions. So, we flick back to Own It to remind ourselves that this is happening whether we like it or not and we can't stay looping in the emotion.

It is important to face and process every emotion as it occurs. Our emotions compound, and if we don't face and process them, they will build and build. Our fuse will get shorter and shorter until at some point the emotions will explode and force us to face and process them. This often happens when we least expect it or want it. So, identify each emotion as it arises, and understand what the core emotion is that you are feeling right now.

The worst thing you can do is to try to convince yourself or other people that the worst-case scenario won't happen. Why? Because it absolutely could happen, and our mind knows that it's a possibility!

There is no script or blueprint on how to react to situations so it's best to embrace the emotions and the process. Allow your mind to wander through the emotions ensuring that you bring them back and take ownership of reality regularly.

Think of as many possible outcomes as possible (including the worst-case scenario) then ask yourself, 'What will I do if that does happen?'

We need to mitigate the risks and understand in our mind what we will do should each possible outcome occur. While our mind doesn't have the actual answer, it knows what it will do regardless of what occurs.

Remember that there is no such thing as a bad emotion. Simply look at the appropriateness and severity of the emotion and ask yourself, 'Is this emotion appropriate for this situation? Is the severity level of how I am feeling this emotion appropriate?' I like to say, 'Face the emotions but don't unpack your bags and stay there.'

Let's look at where Face It comes into play in real-life situations:

- *System changes:* Our emotions during a system change in the workplace can be very mixed. Our old system or process might be clunky or have many downfalls, but the risk of implementing a new system comes with potential errors and a lot of training and will be more of a hindrance than help to begin with. Our emotional brain starts to fire with feelings of fear of the unknown, failure or inability to understand; it could be an emotional feeling of upcoming chaos and become overwhelming. The thought of change alone is enough to trigger many of the emotions based on our relationship with change. We are losing the familiarity of our old system regardless of how good or bad it is. Some people might be really excited about the new system and the upcoming change. Either way, we are always feeling an emotion and those emotions require facing and processing. Understand what it is that you are feeling, and why you are feeling it, so that you can move on.

- *A new job:* A new job can bring with it a rollercoaster of emotions. Excitement at a new beginning but also nervousness. Curiosity around the people and the work environment. Fear in every area. Anger that this is even happening. The first day that we walk into the new environment we can jump through these emotions with speed and feel so good one moment and really be struggling the next. This is a common response. Every one of these emotions has a place or something that is driving it. Ignoring them is not helpful — understanding why we are feeling this way and what we can put in place to take control of the emotion is what will help us through.

- *Reading this book:* The emotions may have begun as soon as you picked up the book. Then, as you started to read the book, there's the fear of remembering everything you read or knowing how to make it happen. The realisation that you thought you were quite emotionally intelligent in areas only to realise that maybe you're not. The noise of the environment around you and your ability to focus and take the information in. Your emotions towards me as an author: 'Do I like her writing style? Is it what I expected?' Excitement at the relatability and the thought of how you will implement the learnings. All the emotions that can fly by in seconds or get stuck in your head. Either way, each one must be felt and processed to move on.

To Face It: face the emotion, process it and move forward.

## Ask

What emotions are currently looping in your mind that you can't seem to get past? Have you faced those emotions, processed them and understood them so that you can move on? Where is your current core emotion coming from? What is triggering you to feel this way? What do you stand to gain in this situation vs what do you stand to lose? What's keeping this emotion in place? How are you feeling about reading this book: excited, unsure, nervous?

# 3. Feel It

Empathy is a key part of this step, but Feel It consists of so much more than just empathy. This is where we get out of our own head and feel the impact we have on the people around us and the impact life is having on them. It's no longer about us. It's about how *they* are feeling right now.

It can be hard to get out of our own head because our inner voice is always going to think about us and what we stand to gain or lose. When we can step outside those self-centred thoughts, we have the opportunity to access some of the greatest skills any leader or human being could have. Our greatest leadership skills come under this area as we learn to understand what makes each of the people around us tick and empathise with them. It's about noticing the differences between other people and what makes them different from us. Importantly, understanding that 'different' is a good thing and is required to achieve balance within any team or group of people. Having a team of identical people and skills doesn't bring diverse thinking or achievements. It's about knowing how to empower them and what motivates each person to reach peak performance based on their drivers, to really help them to become the best they can be.

Feel It is the ability to:

- read the energy of a room and the unspoken signs from other people's body language

- be empathetic and recognise the emotion that other people are feeling; recall the last time we felt that emotion; and avoid the worst thing that someone could do or say, and instead go with the best thing someone could do or say, when that emotion is present

- understand what makes other people tick, what their drivers are and how to empower them

- know that it's not always about us. Sometimes the change is a massive improvement for other people.

This step is about putting ourselves aside and focusing on the people around us and how we can help them.

Let's look at how to Feel It:

- *System changes:* Rarely will a system change be a win in every area for every person. New systems are brought in for a reason, but they are likely to go with the 80/20 rule: 80 per cent of the changes will be improvements, 20 per cent will be disadvantages. Eighty per cent of people will have a better experience, 20 per cent of people will have the same or a diminished experience. Either way, the benefits of the new system should overall be greater or should fix a problem. This might mean we are in that 80 per cent of people who have a better experience — but sometimes we won't be. Sometimes it might do nothing or add extra minutes to our tasks, but we understand it's not all about us. Maybe the improvement for the customer is 10 fold and that's what we want to see. Maybe there is another department that saves 20 minutes per transaction so adding two minutes to our transaction is still a gain overall for the company. Maybe it's an improvement for our transactions and department, which is why we pushed for it, but we can now see it's a nightmare for the customer. Take the time to understand the bigger picture. Get out of your own head and look at the people around you. Think about what's in it for them and how they are impacted by the new system. What can you do to improve the impact on those around you?

- *A new job:* Being in a new job impacts everyone around us too. The new team and organisation that we've joined has to get to know us. The culture will have been impacted because culture is the outcome of a group of people interacting and when the people in that group changes, so does the culture. Our family and friends will be impacted by any change in conditions with the new job and they will be on the receiving end of our emotions based on the new job. Again, this is when we realise it is not just about us. We've owned it and faced it, now is the time to understand how the people around us are impacted by our new job — what can we do to support and help them through this?

- *Reading this book:* At some point while reading this book, you might read something and think, 'Ahh, *this* person really needs to read this or *this* person will really benefit from knowing this — how can I help them now that I know this?' You might have a sledgehammer moment where you realise the impact you've been having on others isn't emotionally intelligent and start to wonder how you can improve in this space to help them. I once had a person in a workshop say that they hadn't spoken with their sister for over two years and, on reflection, they had realised they weren't emotionally intelligent in the situation either and the role that they played was just as big as the role their sister played. Ultimately, our eyes are opened to the people around us and the impact we are having on them. It's all about them and how they feel.

Feel the impact on the people around you!

## Ask

How well do you know the people you work with (especially those you lead) and their drivers? How can you leverage the strengths of each person and create a balanced skill set team that complement and challenge each other? Are empathy and empowerment something you are doing well? What can you work on today to better understand how other people are feeling?

# 4. Ask It

Ask It is all about the way we communicate. The part of our brain that provides logic and analysis comes into play. The emotional brain is known to fire questions at us during step 2, but by the time we reach step 4, we are in control of our emotions. We understand and have engaged the people around us and we are ready to bring logic into play.

Ask It is about asking the right questions but, more importantly, answering the questions that other people are potentially asking us. We start to ask the when, how, who and what questions. We want to know exactly what needs to happen to achieve the outcome: who needs to be involved; how each person will be involved and how they will do it; and when each step is happening.

Ask It is driven by the logical brain. It can't be one-sided; it must be open and effective. It must consist of genuine questions asking for an answer. If we ask for feedback, it's actually meaning it, listening and responding to the feedback provided. It's at this stage that we consult and engage other people into the conversation — especially those who will be impacted — to get a bigger picture. Be careful not to ask for input because you think you have to, then totally ignore everything that is provided. This depletes trust, and people will stop providing input if this happens. Ask for the input because you are truly interested, acknowledge the feedback received, discuss the outcomes and communicate clearly.

So, what are some examples of Ask It?

- *System changes:* The logically driven questions came into play and we started to ask questions like, 'When will the system go live? Who will be providing training? How will that training be delivered? What is the process if errors occur? Are there reference materials for troubleshooting?' By now, our emotions are under control — we now need to know how exactly this is going to work. Brushing over these questions from other people will delay their acceptance. Let them ask the questions and answer them all!

- *A new job:* This is when our actual training or onboarding starts to occur, or we ask our new manager for the expectations of our role, the dress code, the pay cycle, opening hours or the process for obtaining leave. These are logical questions that we require answers to, so we can do our job.

- *Reading this book:* The book is designed to ask you questions and trigger some logical action thinking along the way. Challenge yourself as to why you are reading the book, what the purpose is behind your commitment, what value and actions you will take away, how you can not only increase your EI but also increase EI within the workplace and in interactions with people. You might have questions for me, and I always encourage you to find me on LinkedIn or contact me through my website. I am genuinely always happy to chat.

Ask It is about asking the right logical questions and answering the questions being asked of you.

## Ask

How well do you Ask It? Do you allow the people around you to ask their questions before pushing full steam ahead? How can you improve your interactions with others to provide time for questions to be asked and discussions to be had to make them more efficient and more effective?

# 5. Drive It

Let's make it happen! Drive It is when the rubber hits the road — this is the action and progress step. This is the implementation. It's at this point that we are good with the situation, we've processed the emotions, we've owned it, faced it, felt it and asked it, and now we are ready to Drive It and move on. This sounds like the simplest part of the process, but unfortunately, we are not always great at the implementation. Workplaces are usually not short on great ideas but struggle to implement the ideas. It's this last step that puts everything into play.

We work with the chemicals (serotonin, dopamine, endorphins, oxytocin and cortisol) in our head to create motivation and achieve the desired outcome. It's about working smarter, not harder, and leveraging the natural ways our brain works. It's about doing what we say we are going to do and being efficient while doing it. Being in control of where we choose to spend our time and doing it wisely.

Emotions can resurface here, and we might be so excited that we want everything to happen immediately. A bit like Veruca Salt from the movie *Charlie and the Chocolate Factory* saying, 'I want it, Daddy, and I want it now' and then we end up with nothing at all because the greed and want was unrealistic. Or hesitation and fear could hold us back from this final step and even drag us all the way back to step 2 to face the emotions again.

At step 5 we start:

- working smarter, not harder, to increase efficiencies and approach the implementation from the best possible angle
- minimising any disruptions, blockers and limitations from impacting
- doing what it takes to look, move forward and make it happen!

Examples of Driving It might be:

- *System changes:* Drive It is when the team is ready for rollout or receiving the system changes. Or the first 90 days have been reached and the team realises it's not really that bad and, yes, the advantages do outweigh the disadvantages.
- *A new job:* At step 5 you start your new job or onboarding has finished and you ease into the role. It's the point at which there is some form of implementation action completed with progression forward.
- *Reading this book:* You finish reading the book but then the real work starts: it's time to implement the learnings. How do you bring this to life? This

is where you ask yourself what you stand to gain by implementing new skills and becoming more emotionally intelligent in situations vs what you stand to lose if you don't do anything.

Drive It is the action step. Be efficient and make it happen!

## Ask

Do you do what you say you are going to do? What goals have you set for the next 12 months? Why are these goals important to you? What will potentially stop you from achieving them? How will you ensure this doesn't happen and how will you achieve your desired outcome?

The EI process provides us with a structure and a common language to better understand the steps our mind goes through and how emotionally intelligent we are in every situation. Understanding the process for ourselves provides opportunities for our own personal EI growth and progress. Understanding the process for others creates the ability to individually identify how each team member is coping and what it will take to help them move forward. This is a fantastic leadership skill that is evident in an emotionally intelligent workplace.

## Chapter reflection

- The EI process moves through five steps: Own It, Face It, Feel It, Ask It and Drive It.

- The first two steps are completely in our own head and all about us. It's at step 3 that we get out of our head and start involving the people around us.

- This process is evident in every single thing we do.

- On reflection of understanding the EI process, where do you see this process occurring within your workplace? Which steps are done well as opposed to those done not so well (or completely missed)?

# Chapter 2

# MASTERING THE EI PROCESS

Every situation and every person is different, so to master the five-step EI process, our levels of awareness and adaptability are key.

Be aware of the variances that will occur through:

- the speed at which each person moves through the process
- the EI skill level of each person and their ability to progress through the process
- leaders identifying that people are at different stages at different times and will therefore require different levels of support and leadership
- the size and time sensitivity of the situation
- the process becoming habitual and losing meaning.

Our ability to adapt to each of these variances influences the success of not only the process but also the ultimate outcome.

Let's look at how to build the skills to be adaptable and master the process!

# Speed: I feel the need!

We all go through this process daily, sometimes many times a day, but it's the speed at which we move through the process that differs. Some of us move through Own It, Face It, Feel It, Ask It and Drive It in a matter of minutes; some of us take hours, weeks, months or even years. Some of us, unfortunately, never make it through and tend to get caught looping in our own head around Own It and Face It.

A great leader — correction: a great person — understands how to identify the step of the process that each person is at and recognises what is required to support them to move through each step and on to the next step. We know that every person and every situation requires a slightly different approach, and being a great leader or great human being is having the ability to adapt to the need of the person and situation. A blanket approach is not going to work, and this is the same when it comes to the EI process. Expecting others to align to our speed and ability to go through the process is self-centred and unrealistic. Our speed will also change depending on the situation and our comfort levels.

Take a step back and observe what people are saying, what they are doing and how they are feeling. Use these observations to get a better understanding of what step of the process this fits into. You might have 80 per cent of people progressing through the process at similar speeds and following how you are leading. We meet the other 20 per cent at their step of the process. Listen and discuss what it is that they need in order to move to the next step. When we tailor our leadership and support based on what is needed, it will increase the speed at which we can align everyone involved and achieve the ultimate outcome.

## Making progress

In chapter 1, I spoke about looping back and forth between Own It and Face It, worrying about the emotions and the 'what ifs', finding it hard to accept the reality that this is actually happening and feeling like we do not have any control over the situation. This looping can happen at any of the five steps.

I was working with an organisation that does the most amazing work for the community. They are super passionate about the difference they make to women's health, and their empathy levels are sky high for their patients. Based on this, the third step, Feel It, is a strength for them. But as we spoke, I realised it was a weakness as well.

Internally, when they were looking to make any decisions about change, they were progressing through the first two steps with ease but getting stuck looping in step 3. Their level of Feel It had them wanting to please everyone, to have everyone in agreeance and on board before progressing. The chances of getting hundreds of people to all agree is pretty slim, but the strong 'Feel It' within them was putting everyone's feelings as a number one priority and they were stuck looping with no progress years later. Yes, it's important to go through each step, but it's equally important to be emotionally intelligent enough to know not everyone will agree. Provide the opportunity for everyone to have a voice, but be decisive! Being emotionally intelligent includes being able to make a decision. It's great to hear everyone and let them be involved in the brainstorming and solutions but, equally, a great leader makes the final decision so progress can be made.

It's the same approach as that needed for looping or lacking progress in Ask It: saying that there are always more questions to ask, research to be done or answers to provide. Or looping or lacking progress in Drive It by holding off implementation until everything is perfect, including the timing. Be realistic, and create the balance between engagement, involvement and being decisive to achieve progress.

## Different stages, different support

During COVID, I saw something fascinating happen. Leaders were getting stuck in Feel It. Leaders who cared too much! Is that even a thing? Stay with me while I explain.

When the pandemic first kicked in, these amazing leaders stood up and acted, ensuring their teams were set up to work from home, had everything they needed to do their jobs and had the support required, and they did a brilliant job. Given they were then leading hybrid and remote teams, there was concern around keeping the teams interacting and engaged, and maintaining the culture. Some leaders leveraged online technology, setting up Microsoft (MS) Teams or Zoom virtual meetings each morning so that the team could connect with each other, say good morning and set up for the day, similar to what they would be doing should they all be in the same location together.

This worked so well that they then decided to set up another MS Teams or Zoom call in the afternoon prior to everyone finishing to wrap up the day, know where everyone landed and say goodbye. Which was great.

Then someone suggested a check-in just before lunch would be handy, so they would know who's going to lunch at what times and ensure that there were always people covering or handling work and queries. Then what about just a quick one at the end of the lunch period as well to provide an update now everyone is back — and, on another note, we could have a MS Teams whiteboard on our screens all day to chat and be in contact with each other.

For those people who were still in the Face It step, this was exactly what they needed. They needed support, care, check-ins and contact while they faced their emotions and concerns. The leaders were providing the support and interaction required to help them in the Feel It stage.

However, those who were already at Drive It were driven mad! 'Another meeting? Why do we need another meeting? Are you serious? When will I get time to do my job? Enough already! I'm fine; just let me get on with my job!'

The frustration was real. These people in Drive It had been through the process and were coping. They were already okay and just wanted to get on with things. For some people in Drive It, it created concern and doubt. They started to wonder and fear, thinking 'What do they know that I don't? Maybe this is a bigger deal than I first thought? Maybe I should be more worried than I currently am?' For some of these people, it was enough to drag them back through the process all the way back to Face It and they were again faced with multiple emotions, fears and concerns now looping in their own heads.

Never would I say to stop or not care about someone. As human beings, this is something we should be doing, and doing well. What I am saying, is yet again, it's not about us. Understand what step each person is up to and what they need from us to proceed. Adapt your approach and style to the person in front of you and their needs. If they are already in Drive It, let them continue. Don't create problems that don't exist.

## Time sensitivity

I was in Brisbane, Australia delivering the EI process as part of a workshop for a large hospital group. There were about 150 people in the room, and they were made up of handpicked people across all roles, including surgeons, medical practitioners, clinicians and support teams. I had explained the EI process and was in the midst of talking through how to master the process when one of the surgeons raised their hand and said:

'Amy, I get it, it's nice. But we haven't got time for that! As surgeons, we Own It, Face It then turn to our teams and say, 'Drive It'.

One of the other surgeons agreed and she said:

'Amy, he's right. As nice as it is — and I see what you are trying to do here — it's just not realistic.'

At this point, one of the support team turned to them both and said:

'And that's the problem.'

What was happening was that the surgeons were so used to moving fast in decisions that once they had Owned It, Faced It and had it right in their head, they would turn to their teams, pushing them to Drive It. It just needed to be done. Meanwhile, Feel It and Ask It were totally being skipped and the support team, who were not on board yet, were left behind thinking, 'Hang on, do you know the impact this is going to have on our processes, the patient, the front line? Did you consult or ask anyone from our area for feedback before making this decision? Was anyone engaged in the process before the decision was made? How long has it been since you were on the front line? Before we move forward, I have a list of questions that I need to ask and that need to be answered so we know how to proceed.'

Skipping step 3, Feel It, and step 4, Ask It, is unfortunately a common occurrence in many organisations, leaving the team around them not onboard, pushing back or disengaged. While we feel like we don't have time to Feel It and Ask It, if we don't spend the time upfront, we will be dragged back there by teams that are not onboard. We spend so much time trying to get them onboard, moving forward or doing it correctly afterwards, that if we had done it correctly in the first place, we would have saved time and a lot of frustration.

I was sharing this story with a property development group a few months later in Perth, Australia. They are a long-standing client who had some tension between their project design team and their sales and marketing team. The project design lead spoke up and said he agreed with the surgeons in the story, telling me that he knew my teachings, was a big fan but sometimes there just isn't time. He shared a story from the week prior where he was on a phone call and had to make a multimillion-dollar decision there and then. He didn't have time to see how 'sales and marketing felt about it or if they had any questions'.

At this point, the head of the sales team spoke up, saying, 'And you made the wrong decision!' The tension in the air was so thick you could cut it.

I could certainly understand where they were both coming from. I truly get it. Let's be realistic for a minute: there will always be situations where we have time sensitivity and have to make decisions on the spot. This is going to happen.

So, I asked the project design lead if, after having made the decision and ended the call, he could have picked up the phone, sent an email, or better yet, gone and spoken to the sales and marketing team and told them he had to make a quick decision. He could have said, 'Here are the things I considered from your team's point of view and how it might be impacted. Here are the questions I asked. Did I get it right?' Then the sales and marketing team could have answered 'yes' or 'no'. They might have given him a couple of extra considerations or questions to ask the next time this happened to further assist him with making the decision.

I asked him, 'Would you have had time to do that?'

He responded with 'yes'. I asked the sales and marketing team if this would have helped them. With a resounding yes, they said it all comes down to communication: 'We just want communication and to be on the same page.'

There isn't always time for an in-depth or proactive Feel It and Ask It. Sometimes we learn by reflecting for next time. In saying that, keep in mind that the Feel It and Ask It process can literally be completed by asking two questions:

1. How are you feeling about this situation/process?
2. Do you have any questions?

If we don't make the time, we will be forced to be reactive with people who are not yet on board, cause people tension, and add to conflict between teams that aren't on the same page. This often takes a lot more time and is harder than doing the two steps upfront. Saying that we don't have time for it is a cop out! We all have the same amount of time; it's simply whether we see it as a priority.

As the expression goes, 'Choose your hard'. Is it being proactive or being reactive? What this means is that you will have a hard or difficult challenge at some point of the process: do you want to address it by being proactive or reactive? Either way, one will be required and when it is forced upon us to fix something that is 'broken' it tends to take a lot longer and is a lot harder than doing it right the first time.

## Making it meaningful

Processes, templates and steps make things easier to remember and easier to implement. When we're provided with a process of any kind, there is a risk or trap we can easily fall into, losing the true meaning of why we are doing something.

What I mean by this is when we learn something new it gets stored short term in our hippocampus, then transferred over to our long-term memory or habitual part of our mind during deep NREM sleep. When this occurs, it becomes familiar or a habit. When something becomes a habit, it can very easily detach from purpose and meaning. We tend to find ourselves going through the steps because we know that's what we should do, but the care factor really isn't there. The meaning slowly fades away and it becomes about ticking boxes to know, or be able to say, that we have done it. As we pass these processes or habits onto others, sometimes we fail to explain the 'why' behind them. They become something we simply do that no-one really understands or questions — it's just 'the way we do it'. I'm sure we have all been there in the workplace.

Initiatives, projects and change tend to take on parts of the EI process but are frequently just box ticking without it being meaningful.

Have you ever been witness to or part of a change process where the proposed change was put out to the teams for consultation? This consultation period tends to go for a maximum of two weeks, and everyone is asked for feedback, thoughts, concerns and the like during the consultation period. It's a great way to add extra value to the Feel It and Ask It steps — except when it doesn't.

Too often we see this process implemented and the teams take their time to provide and send feedback. Really tap into their thoughts, experience, knowledge and ideas. The consultation period ends and then everyone receives confirmation that the consultation period has finished and everything that was proposed is moving forward with no mention whatsoever of any of the feedback provided by the teams.

Teams will feel they have been burned and will only do this so many times before they reach the point of losing all care factor and won't provide any feedback again. Why would they, when it's never been listened to or taken into consideration in the past? It was purely a box-ticking exercise and holds no value or meaning.

Whenever we ask for any form of feedback — regardless of how small or how big — acknowledgement of the feedback is always sought after and required.

At the end of consultation, specifically share and acknowledge the feedback received. Confirm that it was all received and considered. Not all feedback is going to be relevant or be likely to change the original decision. Maybe even call out some of the themes and why it was decided that they weren't of concern or didn't alter the outcome.

When the process has lost meaning, we have completely lost the emotional intelligence aspect of the process. The purpose no longer exists and it's a waste of time. We are not truly owning it, facing it, feeling it, asking it and driving it. The process has become words on a page: the stages become something that we go through and simply tick off with no meaning. This defeats the purpose and is in no way emotional intelligence. To truly master and embed the EI process into your work environment, be sure to take the time at every step to maintain the meaning, know why the step is important and the impact it will have if done well vs the impact of it not being done well.

# Chapter reflection

- Awareness and adaptability are key to mastering the EI process.

- Each individual will go through the steps of the process at different speeds with some even struggling to progress at times.

- As great leaders, we meet each individual at their step of the process to understand and offer the support it will take to progress.

- Be realistic! Time sensitivity means some steps might be done in a different order or a more simplified version, but they are always done.

- Successful processes always require meaningfulness and a strong 'why'.

- On reflection of mastering the EI process, how aware and adaptable are you to the people, the situation and the process? Does the EI process hold meaning for you? What can you do to further master the EI process?

# Chapter 3

# THE CONSTANT EVOLUTION

Like many parts of our life today, the EI process isn't a one-off process that provides you with one chance to get it right, and if not, it's too late. We have the luxury of having choices at each step and due to the process being a constant evolution, if it's not done right the first time, as it rolls through again, we have a chance to be more emotionally intelligent and master the process.

The evolution of the EI process restarts every time Drive It gets completed. When someone or something implements the drive stage, the people impacted or involved in any way start back at step 1: own the reality of the situation. This provides the opportunity to reflect on how well the process was previously done, and also provides us with a framework with a common understanding and a contagious common language that helps to take the personal aspect out of ensuring EI is always in play.

Let's have a look at:

- the ways in which the evolution of the process cascades through the layers of our organisation and how we create more emotionally intelligent teams
- the advantage of a common language to embed the EI process
- the power and relatability in frequency
- how every part of the organisation benefits.

# Cascading through the layers

Often decisions are made at a high level in an organisation and the decision is then cascaded down through the layers. Unfortunately, not all people will leverage their EI and go through the five steps of the EI process in every situation. We can't force people to be emotionally intelligent. We can't force people to do anything they don't choose to do. So, when decisions are made at a level higher than us, are we able to still Feel It and Ask It with our teams if it has already been made and we are being told to just Drive It?

Yes, we always have the ability to Feel It and Ask It, regardless of what stage we are at in the communications or process. This is because the EI process is a constant evolution and starts again once a decision has been made.

I was working with a government-owned business and was speaking at one of their conferences. Rosters were a challenging problem for the leaders as they were impacting many of the team members, resulting in complaints and resignations. They mentioned how the decision regarding the rosters was made at the very top of the organisation and by the time it got to their level, they had no say — just a directive to do it. Their organisational structure is not different from any other organisational structure in that there is someone sitting right at the top who is the ultimate decision maker, then cascading layers of authority, roles and people.

This top decision maker has several people reporting directly to them, creating the second level of management, and the organisational structure flows from there with the second level having direct reports from the third level, the third level having direct reports from the fourth level and so on until they reach the community. Figure 3.1 (overleaf) illustrates this process.

When the process begins at the very top level, we hope that the top decision maker leverages their emotional intelligence and owns the reality that this is a problem and requires action. All the emotions relating to this would then surface and the top decision maker would need to face each emotion, acknowledge and process it so that they can clear it and move forward. Those emotions might be frustration that this is occurring, concern for the impacted team members, concern for the community due to resignations and resources or relief that now is the time to finally create a solution to this ongoing problem. Regardless of the emotions, they must be faced.

Once this occurs, the top decision maker gets out of their own head and engages their direct reports in a conversation of Feel It. This might include open discussions around the current state, possible solutions, a better understanding of how it works and the impacts, and then everyone's thoughts, concerns and opinions in relation to the challenge.

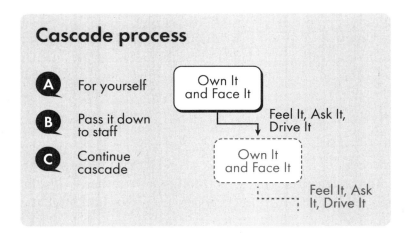

## Example

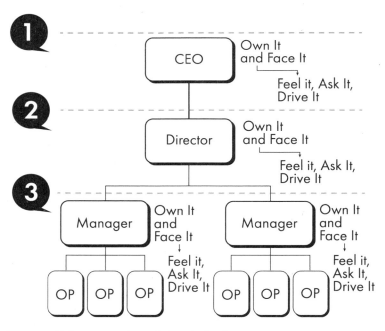

**Figure 3.1:** cascading through the layers

The length of time and depth of discussion is up to those participants involved.

Ask It is when the logical questions kick in for both the top decision maker and their direct reports. 'What is the core problem here? Why is it important and what is the impact? How will we fix it? Who will be involved? When is the best time for this to occur?' Once all questions are asked and answered, at some point the top decision maker has to pull rank, make a final decision around the rosters and give direction to Drive It.

We know that any decision made isn't necessarily going to be agreed upon by everyone involved but either way, a decision has to be made and agreed upon as a leadership team. As leaders, it is their responsibility that once the decision is made, they must be 100 per cent on board with the outcome. The slightest crack or hesitation that they are not 100 per cent in agreement or on board will be picked up on by the teams and they too won't be on board, and this will cascade through every level.

Once the Drive It step has occurred, the time for that layer of leaders to challenge and question is over, and the EI process starts again.

It's now time for the second level managers to return to step 1 and own the reality of the situation and that the decision has been made. Fresh emotions will now arise based on what they think of the final decision. They might be happy with the outcome, or it might not have been where they were hoping it would land, and frustration might be occurring. Regardless of the emotion, it's time to face all emotions, and acknowledge and process them so they can get out of their own head and move forward into Feel It and Ask It, to cascade the decision to their direct reports and so on through the layers of the organisation.

This is what should happen, but quite often we don't get out of our own head. We don't restart the process and Own It and face the reality of the decision ready to Feel It and Ask It with our teams. We turn around to our direct reports, frustrated at the outcome — because it is not what we think it should be — or we're simply still in the Drive It step in our head and just tell them to Drive It without even attempting to Feel It or Ask It.

Our direct reports are not on board or satisfied with this and start to push back, trying to get us to Feel It and understand the impact it will have on them and the frontline. They will try to Ask It to get answers to all their concerns and questions. They aren't aware of the previous conversations or process that has occurred; all they are hearing is 'just do it'. But instead of us following the evolution of the process, starting at step 1 and moving through each step with them, we respond with 'I've tried already; there's no use, just do it!'

Our direct reports, now as frustrated as we are, sadly turn around and do the same thing to the next layer down. They loop in their Own It and Face It and turn to the next layer down telling them to Drive It. 'There's no use. I've tried — just do it!' This process continues down through the layers or ranks until it hits the community, and they push back only to be told, 'It is what it is.'

There was a resounding agreement at the conference that this is exactly what happens, but what other choice did they have when the decision was already made?

This is the massive benefit of the evolution of the process as it cascades. Regardless of where we sit in the decision-making and communication process, there is always the chance to Feel It and Ask It because the process starts again each time a decision is made. We are owning the new decision, the new reality of the situation. When we turn to our direct reports and communicate the decision, we let them know the current reality of the situation, but we can still ask them: 'How do you *feel* about this? Do you have any concerns? Are there any questions you would like to ask? Given we all must own the reality of the situation, how do we work together to make it work? What do we have control over here and what approach will we take together?'

To pass the buck and say, 'I had no choice by the time it reached my level' is wrong and lacks EI. We always have a choice. Just because we don't like the reality of the situation, doesn't mean the people who made the decision weren't being emotionally intelligent. They could have been very emotionally intelligent and what they landed on was the best outcome from going through the process. Maybe they weren't emotionally intelligent at all and didn't go through the process. This is irrelevant. When it becomes our communication, we always have the opportunity to start the emotional intelligence process again and reset at our level.

When we look at some organisations where the overall culture isn't great, we can still see pockets of teams in random parts of the organisation that do have great culture. This is because those leaders, regardless of their level and contribution to the decision-making process, always remember to start the EI process again and help their team to progress through all five steps with them.

It's the same with organisations where the overall culture is fantastic but there are pockets of teams where the culture is not great because those leaders are choosing not to involve the EI process at their level. They are seeing the process as a linear, one-time process that only happens at the very top. This is definitely not the case; we always have a choice to be emotionally intelligent.

# A common language

One of the biggest challenges across communication is speaking the same language. The evolution of the EI process creates a common language across people and workplaces. Being able to refer to EI within every part of the organisation using the five steps of the EI process becomes relatable across the organisation and builds a greater acceptance. If a company really wants to embed EI into their culture and what they do, my first suggestion is always to get it on every agenda and use the same common language. This common language also provides an easier way to approach what could be a difficult conversation.

I had finished running my EI program for an executive leadership team in the Asia–Pacific (APAC) region and when we all came together for a follow-up session, the leaders shared a story that in the weeks that followed the original program, they were having a meeting about a change that was going to be rolled out across the region when one of the team said, 'Hang on, we haven't felt it or asked it'. Given it was common language, it caused all the attendees at the meeting to pause and think back to the process, the importance of these two steps and the potential consequences of not doing them. They agreed it hadn't been completed properly and everything shifted to ensure Feel It and Ask It had been completed.

Interrupting a conversation, a change or decision based on a lack of EI, consideration or communication with the people affected is often not an easy or smooth thing to do. It can become quite personal or create a defensive reaction due to discomfort or fear. When we have a common language, it takes the personal side out of it and puts us all on the same page with the same understanding. It becomes easier to question and raise concerns in a safe environment as the alignment and agreement to the process has already been made in the past; we are simply realigning.

## Frequency illusion

As this evolution gains traction across the organisation, it becomes part of the processes and eventually part of the culture. We start to see the process and common language in everything we do individually and as a team.

You know what it's like when you are looking to purchase a new car and all of a sudden you see the same car everywhere! This is selective attention, or a cognitive bias called the 'frequency illusion', also known as the Baader-Meinhof phenomenon. It means that our self-awareness has peaked after learning something and our subconscious mind tends to be more aware of it and sees/experiences it more often. Sometimes we even believe that it is not our selective attention, but that it is occurring more often and therefore it gives more reassurance to our learnings that it is important.

As the EI process grows across more people in our workplace, we start to realise just how common it is and how much sense it makes. It becomes obvious in every situation, grows so that it's not just a frequency illusion but an actual increase in frequency. A 'given' rather than a 'nice to have'. It's a natural process that helps us to understand the key factors of EI and how they fit into day-to-day occurrences. The more understanding and identifying that occurs, the more emotionally intelligent our processes and our workplaces become.

## Who really benefits?

With evolution comes growth and development. But how do we measure the real value and benefit in the EI process as it evolves?

This isn't a trick question. It's also not rocket science. We know that everything that exists in our world is due to human intervention. The effectiveness of the human intervention will always directly influence the outcome of any situation. Our IQ is the 'what we know and what we can do', while our EI is the 'how and why of what we do'. When it comes to workplaces, how we make people feel, how we deliver our tasks and meet our role requirements, how we communicate, why we do what we do and the purpose of everything we do directly influences the success of the organisation.

**This means the EI process is, and always has been, the core driver of our bottom line, products/services and the customer.**

We don't get to choose whether we have time for emotional intelligence or whether we will bring it into play. The same as we don't get to choose whether we have time for leadership. EI is happening regardless of whether we want it to or not. If the focus and priority aren't there to do EI well, then there is a good chance it's being done poorly.

How well each and every one of us leverages and grows our EI will always impact the success of our workplaces.

So, there is no downside to being emotionally intelligent in the workplace. This is no disadvantage when we embed the EI process in all that we do. There are only endless advantages.

When it comes to focusing and prioritising EI, as Oprah says, we are all winners! 'You get a car, you get a car, you get a car, everybody gets a car!'

# Chapter reflection

- The EI process never ends. It is a constant evolution that continues to circle back and start again with each decision made.

- We all have the opportunity to implement the EI process no matter what layer of the organisation we are in. It's never too late to follow the process.

- Having a common language across conversations and embedded in agendas makes it easier to create an emotionally intelligent culture.

- The EI process can be found everywhere and the more we increase the frequency of use, the faster it moves from a frequency illusion to reality.

- There are only endless advantages to implementing the EI process in your workplace.

- On reflection of the constant evolution of the EI process, where are the opportunities for you to bring the process into your team, workplace or even your life?

Part II

# CHANGE INTELLIGENCE

There is no doubt that change is one of the most talked-about topics in the workplace — and even in life. Statistics from the *Walk Me* blog highlight that a whopping 96 per cent of organisations are undergoing some form of transformation or change right now but only 34 per cent of change initiatives succeed. Let's just stop and think about that for a moment. Think about all the change that is currently happening in your workplace. Not just the 'big stuff'. I mean all the small process changes, operational changes, environmental changes, people changes and strategic changes. Sixty-six per cent of these changes will not be successful ... that's incredible!

It's an absolute given that change is occurring and will continue to occur. It also seems to be a given that people are expected to love and embrace change, but do we really have to love and embrace every form of change?

I can remember being asked a question at a keynote about five years ago: 'Amy, change has been around for as long as we have been. Why are people so obsessed and harping on about it so much in workplaces today?' They had a valid point: change comes with being a human being. It's always been happening and always will be, as sure as time moves. But what we are noticing these days is that the change we are experiencing is frequently on a much larger scale than it previously was.

In the past, change that was rolled out in a new workplace may have been a slight process or product change, a new brand of paper for the photocopier — or a big change such as getting a new photocopier! Change was always there but it was less frequent and less impactful. Today, it's all about rapid acceleration in the pace of change and the size of each of the changes. The digital transformation spending alone for workplaces worldwide will reach $2.8 trillion in 2025 (an increase from 0.96 trillion in 2017, according to *TeamStage*). We can only imagine the extent of change this will continue to fund into the future. Change is getting faster and bigger and will continue that way — I'm sure that isn't new information to anyone.

But it's not the size and speed of change that I want to talk about — it's our change intelligence (CI). That is, the relationship we have with change, the relationship that change has within our emotional intelligence and therefore the way we respond and adapt to change. Change itself is not usually the problem — it's the way in which it is communicated and implemented, and the lack of adapting and aligning our mind with the change that can cause change to be unsuccessful.

In part II, we will dive into the relationship between change and our mind. We will look at the transition and EI process that happens in our neural pathways, as our mind is faced with something different from what we are familiar with or something that is not expected. It is completely okay to not love change; consistency has its place. I'm going to help you understand what occurs in the mind and the transitions of change intelligence before acceptance is reached.

So, let's work with the mind and its process rather than jumping straight to 'selling' the change and trying to convince people to love it upfront.

# Chapter 4

# OUR RELATIONSHIP WITH CHANGE

Change management hit the workplace radar in the 1990s and started to be seen as a formalised department, role and process throughout organisations in the 2000s. 'Change' became the new trend word, and a frequent question asked in interviews was, 'How are you with change?', which was generally met with a resounding, 'I'm great — I love change' from interviewees, regardless of how they really feel about change.

To get the job and be successful there was an expectation that you should love change and if you don't already, then embrace it and learn to love it really quickly! Saying you preferred consistency over change is unlikely to get you the job and is at times frowned upon as if not loving change was a bad thing.

Loving or hating change, or being good or bad at change, shouldn't be so clear-cut. Instead, let's look at change on a scale between 1 and 10 (as in figure 4.1), with 1 being rarely changing and preferring consistency, to 10 being loving change and sometimes changing for the sake of changing (not always a great thing). There isn't a right or wrong end of the scale to be at. Like EI, CI is first about awareness. It's about knowing where we sit on that scale based on our wirings and working with these wirings rather than against them.

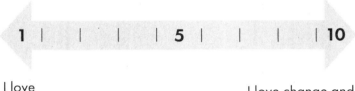

I love
consistency and
I am great at it!

I love change and
sometimes change
for change's sake!

**Figure 4.1:** the change scale

Our relationship with change, like everything else in our mind, is a reflection of our wirings. These have been created based on our values, beliefs, long-term memories, experiences and the environment in which we have been raised.

For some of us who have been raised in environments of consistent change, this becomes our 'normal' and then not only do we expect it but at times we crave it!

I'm writing this as I sit on a plane eating Doritos Mexicana corn chips. Our relationship with change is comparable to our relationships with travel and spice in our foods. When we travel a lot, it becomes expected and part of our wiring and beliefs that this is what we do: our 'normal'. Arriving at the airport becomes second nature and our body goes into auto mode making our way through check-in and security.

When we have a span of time without travel, we feel a bit lost or like we get 'itchy feet' or find ourselves looking for an excuse to book a plane trip. Something doesn't quite feel right, or we seem bored always being in the same place. Our life feels different, not normal, and can be uncomfortable or take time to adjust to.

Some of us have grown up eating food with spice and our tolerance for chili and pepper has increased as we age to become our 'normal', where others struggle to handle the slightest heat or avoid any form of spicy food. We have our 'normal' spicy level defined in our head and anything outside of that is different or a change. Our mind is constantly assessing what 'normal' is and the more time things happen around us, the more we tend to accept them as 'normal' and therefore expected. This alters the values and beliefs in our minds and our expectations.

Growing up, I changed schools eight times between pre-school and Year 8 (middle school). From Year 8 to the end of my schooling, I was at the same school. So, effectively, I was the 'new girl' eight times in my earlier schooling years. This was tough, but also exciting. It helped to form the foundations of my personality as I wanted to make friends and settle in as fast as possible, not knowing how long it would be before we moved again. Between Year 8 and Year 12, time seemed to take forever! I lost count of how many times I asked my parents if I could move to a different school for obscure reasons when really it was just change that I was craving and lack of change was causing boredom. I was so used to changing schools due to my relationship with change that it felt odd being stuck in the same school. There had been so much consistency in those years that I was craving something new — some sort of change — anything to break the *Groundhog Day* feeling.

Since leaving home at 17, I've moved house seven times, then spent six months travelling around Australia with my (now) husband to then land in Perth, Australia. Add another three more moves before landing in our family home — where we have lived for over 18 years. Needless to say, change was a big part of my 'normal' for a good chunk of my life and without the ongoing moves in the past 18 years, I have craved change in other areas, whether it be job roles, having our babies, travelling, buying new furniture or simply rearranging a room. Based on the change scale, my relationship with change is definitely up towards the 10 end given the early wiring of change being a normal expected part of my life.

If you imagine me in a workplace environment, this isn't always going to be a good thing. I'm always on the lookout for the next 'shiny new toy' to keep me entertained and satisfy my crave for change. While I had a very long tenure at the same company, I changed roles on average every two years looking for the next challenge and learnings. It's great to have people who are career-driven innovators in your team, but a whole team filled with these type of people means a high turnover and consistently training new starters. Every team needs people who love consistency and are happy to come in each day and do the same job, becoming experts in their field. In addition, we also need people across the change scale to balance out the extremities at either end of the scale. We need some people at 3 on the scale, some at 8 and some sitting on the fence at 5 to create challenge and a good balance between innovation and consistency.

It's not about being right or wrong, loving or hating change, it's about understanding that change is happening whether we like it or not — this we have very little, if any, control over. So, how do we ensure we are aware, and understand our wiring and relationship with change, so we can work with the change occurring around us as a balanced team?

## Ask

Where do you currently sit on the change scale? Are you up closer to the 10 and craving change or closer to the 1 with consistency? If you are unsure, think about the decisions that you make during everyday life when you get to choose your preference, for example:

- When you go to your favourite restaurant, do you order the same thing every time or do you try something different?

- Is your haircut and colour pretty much the same as it was five years ago, or do you like to mix it up? (Maybe skip this question if you are lacking hair on your head!)

- What do you eat each day? Is it the same or different? Or is every Tuesday 'Taco Tuesday' and every Friday 'Fish Friday'?

- Are you able to name your favourite song, book, movie, colour, chocolate, drink . . .? (People who love change tend to struggle to name just one favourite.)

- How many places have you lived in since you moved out of the family home?

- How often do you update your wardrobe, furniture, car, phone?

- Do you prefer a job that has new tasks every day or do you prefer to work on the one task for extended periods of time?

Being aware of your answers and where they would sit from 1–10 on the change scale will help you to understand your relationship with change in different circumstances. It's okay if your answers change dramatically in different circumstances — again, there is no right or wrong answer. You might enjoy change a lot more at home than you do at work, and that's totally okay.

**Change intelligence is not setting out to alter your relationship with change but to understand it. Once you understand how you are going to cope and respond in moments of change, you can start to prepare yourself.**

Every change has a trigger driving it and every mind will weigh up 'What do I stand to gain from this change?' vs 'What do I stand to lose?' It is basic risk mitigation and knowing what's in it for you. This is where our growth vs fixed mindset kicks in. With a growth mindset, we always find an opportunity in change by looking at 'What do I stand to gain?' It's the optimistic angle: the glass-half-full approach. Conversely, a fixed mindset tends to have us dwelling on the past, the loss or the negative: the 'What do I stand to lose?' It's the pessimistic angle: the glass-half-empty approach. A fixed mindset would be thinking, 'This won't work', whereas a growth mindset would be thinking 'This could work' or 'What if it does work?' or 'How good would it be if it did work?' or 'How could we make this work?'

This is a very easy tool to challenge our mindset with if we default to being opposed to a change. Simply flip the fixed mindset to a growth mindset. It works on the same principles as writing a gratitude diary every day.

A gratitude diary forces us to think of the things we are grateful for rather than what we don't have. A growth mindset forces us to think of the opportunity in the change. It's unlikely to change our wiring or relationship with change, but it will force our mindset to be more open and likely to accept the change. Remember, we don't have to love the change, but we do have to accept it.

The more information and understanding we have around the change, and our relationship with change, the better we can process the change and put steps or tools in place to move forward with the change rather than fight it and get left behind.

## Don't force change

Change is a bit like having a baby. The lead-up can be huge. It's like riding an emotional rollercoaster. We become obsessed thinking about this baby every second of every day for the duration of the pregnancy. It's all we want to speak about with anyone. Everything we see, do, hear, smell, taste and touch we relate back to the baby. Our baby is the most important thing that is happening in this world right now and what we are going through is huge! We live the ups and downs and the highs and lows of the pregnancy. When the baby is finally born, we are just so relieved they have arrived: we are so proud, and our love is so strong. We look at them and only see the most perfect features and really pure perfection in every way. We take endless photos and share just how much we love them and how perfect our baby is with everyone around us and want everyone to love our baby and think they are perfection too.

This is pretty much change too. When we are leading any form of change, the lead-up is huge, and we also ride an emotional rollercoaster. The scope, ideas and expectations start in a very different place from where they land. The change consumes our thoughts and conversations and we believe it is the most important thing and that everyone should be thinking about and prioritising it right now. We live the ups and downs, the highs and lows and then finally it launches. The relief and pride are so strong. We know the battles and near misses we went through, and we know the outcome might not be perfect but it's so much better than the catastrophe it could have been at many stages. We send endless emails, put up posters and pretty much share how amazing our change is and that everyone should love it.

Meanwhile, other people see in our baby the things that we only see when they are grown up and we look back on baby pictures — when we truly see how big their head was, how their nose looked too big for their face, or that they were a little yellow and alien looking or that cute face they pulled wasn't that cute after all! They compare our baby to their baby, to other people's babies. Our baby isn't their number one love nor their number one obsession and priority. Their lives are continuing to happen, and the birth of our baby is simply something happening in the background.

In fact, the change that has just been implemented was not what they were sold in the beginning. Not what they expected. They haven't experienced the ups and downs and almost catastrophes along the way. They are just seeing the outcome and comparing it to their expectations of what it should look like. It's really not that much of an improvement on the current way they do things (their baby). Sure, there are some benefits, but there are also some disadvantages and annoyances. They don't love our baby. They still love their (old) baby.

We push harder to try to get them to love our baby. We rattle off the advantages — how beautiful our baby is — and we even go as far as to tell them how ugly their baby (old way) is. This triggers emotional hijacks in both of us and we both dig our heals in and go into defence mode fighting for our babies, which we have put so much time, emotion and love into. We are pushing the new change as the best thing ever and they are attached to the way it was before the new change.

Don't try to force someone to love your baby. Don't tell them that their baby is ugly. Don't tell them how bad the old way was and that they just should love everything about the new way. Introduce your baby to them, let them get to know your baby and be involved with your baby, and talk about how your baby will help their baby and they can be friends. Transition and merge the change; it doesn't have to be a hard line between the two worlds.

**Be emotionally intelligent. Don't force change.**

# Types of workplace change

Change comes in all different shapes and sizes in the workplace just as it does in every area of life. While there are many types of change, let's focus on the three main types that occur in the workplace: strategic, innovative and people change. Within each of these three areas, we have planned, unplanned and reactive change:

- *Strategic change:* Strategic change is high-level change that aligns to the business and the strategic plan. It's change at the core of the identity of the organisation that will impact the direction, goals, purpose, focus areas, targets and more. It's generally decided at an executive level and cascaded throughout the organisation. Strategic changes tend to be more planned and long term. This means a lot of thought, discussions, analysis, risk mitigation and mapping have been done to create the change plan since strategic change tends to be big change in both effort and impact.

- *Innovative change*: Innovative change is a new way of doing things. Whether it be systems, processes or products, it is new for the business and seen as an improvement on the way things are currently done, or something that hasn't previously existed. It tends to be forward thinking using new technology, methods or advancements and leverages our creative skills. Innovative change can be a real mix of planned and reactive change. The planned innovative change is the same approach as above, while the reactive tends to occur when something has gone wrong or hasn't worked for the situation or person. We hear things like 'What if we did it this way?' and 'What if we change/improve that with this?' It's in these moments of error or failure that our mind is forced to the edge of chaos to think under pressure on how we can make it work. When this pressure and chaos is occurring, we aren't as likely to overanalyse or be too cautious. We just say things that pop into our head without vetting them, and this is where great ideas can come from. Having reactive change can be a double win as it is solving a live problem and improving things for the future as well. We get to test it outright then and there to see how it will work and to identify ways to improve the change from there.

- *People change*: People change is exactly as it sounds. It's when we have a change in our people through different roles or coming/going from the organisation. Change in people can be one of the toughest because with every person we interact with there is some form of emotional connection. Sometimes this will be a positive connection and sometimes a negative connection — or anywhere in between. The emotions attached to it tend to be more complex as they are two-way emotions between both us and them. When we bring new people into the equation, a new emotional connection also will be formed, but this will take time. People change varies across all three areas of planned, unplanned and reactive. The planned and reactive changes use a similar approach to the above, but it is the unplanned changes that really challenge us. When there is an unexpected resignation or restructure, or new starter, the whole dynamics of the team and organisation shift. We know that our culture is the outcome of a group of people interacting and when that group of people changes, our culture also changes.

## Leader approach: workplace

Our approach to change as leaders should vary depending on whether the change is planned, unplanned or reactive. Figure 4.2 (overleaf) is a guide to approaching and communicating the change, although a great leader is always adaptable and responds to the needs of the person and the situation by remembering to both 'Feel It' and 'Ask It'.

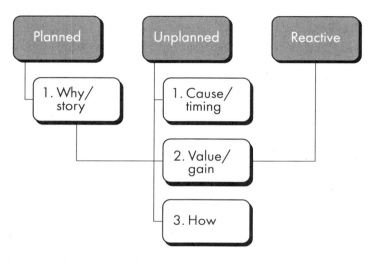

**Figure 4.2:** approaching and communicating a change

The Why/Story behind the change should be shared first and as early as possible. This should be included in the build-up to the change and should have been sourced through a number of different areas and people. That way it is relatable to everyone and they all know how it aligns to them and the role they play. It is the level of the connection to the Why/Story that sets our context for the following steps:

- The Cause/Timing provides the context for change that is unplanned. People need to know what has occurred and what the timing is for this unplanned change.

- The Value/Gain is the ongoing question our mind asks us before we make any decision: 'What do I stand to gain vs what do I stand to lose?' This is the 'sell'! Why should people care? What's in it for them? If these questions are hard to answer, then buy-in will also be hard to obtain.

- The How is our mind needing to fill in the gaps for the fear of the unknown that has just popped into our mind. We want to know exactly how it's going to happen in addition to the 4Ws (what, when, why and who).

As leaders, following this approach helps our minds, and the minds of everyone who will be impacted by the change, to be on the same page.

## Personalities in change

There really are as many personalities as there are people, given every single one of us is wired slightly differently. So, when change occurs, we see an endless number of responses through different people, some of which we attempt to categorise into personality labels. Here are 28 different personalities that can be found through the myriad different change management processes that exist:

- Pioneers
- 'Yes' people
- Champions
- Ambassadors

- Leaders
- Navigators
- Chargers
- Co-pilots

- Supporters
- Early adopters
- Sceptics
- Cave people
- Prisoners
- Saboteurs
- Thieves
- Objectors
- Mutterers
- Critics/Cynics
- Victims
- Militants
- Crowd followers
- Challengers
- Fence sitters
- Followers
- Bystanders
- Worriers
- Passengers
- Resisters

Regardless of how many personality labels, and names given to them, there are, what we really need to understand is whether they sit in the 'Yes, I'm on board', 'No, I'm not on board' or 'Neutral at this stage' category in relation to the upcoming change.

It's a great exercise to discuss this list to establish which category you believe each person fits into. There is likely to be a difference in beliefs and that's completely okay. The purpose of the exercise is the discussion around how many different ways people can react to change. For this reason, I don't worry too much about the personality labels and focus more on the 'yes', 'no' and 'neutral' categories (see figure 4.3). This will also help if you change teams or companies and they use different change management processes: again, you only need to identify whether they sit in the 'yes', 'no' or 'neutral' category.

## *Leader approach: personalities*

Once you are clear on the categories, you will see that the leader approach is slightly different for each because needs differ depending on people's mindsets.

For each of the three personality categories — yes, neutral and no — there are three areas to focus on in order for you and your team to best help each other. You'll find these illustrated in figure 4.3.

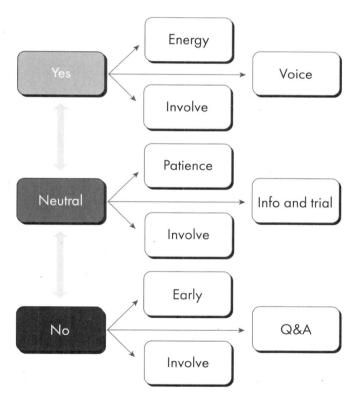

**Figure 4.3:** leader approaches based on personality

Let's run through them.

- *Yes:* The people in the 'yes' category are your
  advocators and supporters. They will have energy
  brimming with positivity and excitement. While
  this can be annoying or frustrating to those who
  aren't in this category, leverage this energy for good
  and get the balance right so they can use their voice
  to support the change. Get them involved! This
  shouldn't mean screeching it from the rooftops
  with placards supporting the change. It should
  be appropriate and effective to match the level of
  change and the emotions that surround the change.
  These people are the ones who can help to educate
  and influence the 'neutral' bucket through Feel It
  and Ask It. They might be too much to let loose
  on the 'no' bucket and when this does happen can
  end up in confrontation, difference of opinions or
  ego-driven conversations. Test the waters first. If
  there is a relationship and emotional connection
  between the 'yes' and 'no' people, an open
  conversation of thoughts, opinions and beliefs may
  be an option, but please monitor this carefully.

- *Neutral:* The people in the 'neutral' category are
  undecided. They might not care or be fazed about
  the change, or they might care so much that they
  are worried about both extremities and be feeling
  quite anxious. Either way, it will take patience to
  understand what is driving the neutral decision and
  the emotions that are attached to it. Provide them
  with more information and even let them test or
  trial any areas they are undecided on, remembering
  that the mind doesn't do well with the unknown.

Offer for them to get involved. This won't be for everyone in this category, but the choice should be theirs. As a leader, you are doing Feel It and Ask It, and one of the great questions to ask is 'What do they want/need to help them decide on how they feel about the change?' Keep in mind that the neutral bucket is most influenced by the people around them, so be observant and aware of who is assisting them.

- *No:* The people in the 'no' bucket believe, for whatever reason, that this change is not right or needed. They will have a strong reason as to why they believe this, and it is our job as leaders to listen and understand this. This group tends to feel 'too hard' or 'too confrontational', so it is common for us to ignore them, hoping the problem will go away, or that they will come around on their own, or we may even try to sweep them under the carpet, so to speak. I would strongly advise against this. The longer we leave or ignore the 'no' bucket, the higher the risk of the no becoming stronger. Early conversations are a must. Conversations should not be one-sided. Let them speak and air their beliefs, concerns or reasoning behind their decision. There will be times when what they say is very valid and maybe we didn't think about or consider that. It could result in a tweak or edit to the upcoming change. Consider having a chat with the 'no' people separately from everyone else as they are highly contagious. Take them into the room 15 minutes before everyone else when communicating a change. Give them the 15 minutes one-on-one to observe their first reactions and ask as many questions as they like. The first reaction can be quite extreme and defensive, and it won't benefit anyone if this reaction is done in front of the whole team (especially the neutral people). The Feel It and Ask It here should be more of a Q&A than us providing more information that may or may not be relevant. Offer for them to get involved as this might help them (or they might not be interested). Either way, if the change is going ahead, help them to Own It, then Face It and move forward into the Feel It, Ask It and Drive It. When a 'no' person shifts to a 'yes' person, these are the most influential people for the 'neutral' people. Neutral people will listen more to someone who has gone from a 'no' to a 'yes' than someone who has always been a 'yes'.

## Ask

How do you approach change with your team? Do you use a 'one-size-fits-all' approach? What opportunities do you have to work with the different personalities, different types of change and people's relationships with change?

Approaching change requires the leader to be adaptable to each person. Without this understanding and approach, you will get some people on board but not everyone. Unfortunately, those not on board tend to be the most vocal so it's always worth the time and effort upfront to increase the acceptance of change by adapting your leadership style.

## Chapter reflection

- Our relationship with change is a sliding scale. It's not about loving or hating change. It's about understanding and accepting it.

- Change should never be forced. Get people involved and allow them to process the change before you push the change.

- There are different types of change and personalities that respond to change in the workplace. The leader approach adapts depending on these types of change and personalities.

- On reflection of relationships with change, identify when a change in the workplace has been influenced or impacted due to team members' relationships and leaders' approaches.

# Chapter 5

# THE CHANGE INTELLIGENCE MODEL

The leadership and workplace market are flooded with change models and all of them provide a slightly different approach to implementing successful change. The model that aligns best with the EI process and the mind is the Bridges Transition Model.

In this chapter, we will look at what the Bridges Transition Model is and how when brought together with the five-part EI methodology, it becomes a change intelligence model that is transformational for change in every workplace.

The book *Managing Transitions: Making the most of change*, written by William Bridges PhD and Susan Bridges, was first published in 1991. The book defines the difference between change and transition with change as being 'the external event or situation that takes place', where transition is the 'inner psychological process that people go through as they internalise and come to terms with the new situation that the change brings about'.

It is very common for organisations to plan for change and have a clear process that is driven to achieve the new outcome, but it is the transition or the human side of the change that is often not addressed or is ignored. However, when we look at the success of change within the workplace, it is heavily dependent on the employee's acceptance, alignment and useability, which is influenced by their ability to transition. So, as William and Susan Bridges assert, 'It isn't the change that will do you in; it's the transitions.'

To attain the transitions, we are reliant on the human mind and how it reacts, so our EI absolutely plays a huge role in the transitions. The transitions themselves aren't enough without the emotional EI working with it alongside them.

The Bridges Transition Model breaks the transitions of change down into these three key steps that people go through:

1. Endings (what currently is)

2. Neutral zone (seedbed for new beginnings)

3. New beginnings (release of energy in a new direction).

These three steps align with the five-step EI process discussed earlier in this book:

1. Own It

2. Face It

3. Feel It

4. Ask It

5. Drive it.

When considering my EI process through the lens of transitions, it takes on a new change intelligence perspective.

It helps us to not only be aware of what is happening, but also to utilise all our EI skills and change intelligence approaches to help us succeed in the transition of the mind and therefore succeed in the change. When transitions are considered with my EI process, it creates a new look and a deeper transition leveraging our EI and the wirings of our mind. Here's how it looks as a three-step process:

1. Step 1: Own and face the loss

2. Step 2: Feel and ask through the liminal space

3. Step 3: Drive the change like a champion.

Figure 5.1 (overleaf) shows the focus areas within each of the steps of the new change intelligence model.

**Figure 5.1:** the change intelligence model

With this new change intelligence model, we bring people and process together. In chapters 6, 7 and 8 we will lift the lid on each step of the model and dive into the meaning, the logic and actions to make change a success.

# Chapter reflection

- Change intelligence is a three-step process. First, we must 'own and face the loss', then we 'feel and ask our way through the liminal' before we 'drive the change like a champion'.

- The process the mind goes through is a key part of change.

- Successful change happens when we bring both the people and the process together.

- On reflection of the change intelligence model, how much focus have you been putting on the people and the process their mind goes through when change occurs?

# Chapter 6

# STEP 1: OWN AND FACE THE LOSS

Step 1 of the change intelligence model is focused on what is happening in each person's mind when they are first impacted by the change.

With every change, regardless of whether it is good, bad or ugly, there is always a loss. Our mind loses something. Whatever it is that we lose, our mind already has the embedded memory and a neural pathway with habits attached. So, when something is removed, our mind struggles to let go of it because it has become part of our 'normal' and standard expectations. We must own this first, face the emotions and get closure.

In this chapter we break down step 1 to understand the initial impact of change, regardless of how amazing it is, and the emotions that are triggered due to the loss that has occurred. Once we recognise and understand this, there needs to be some form of closure to draw the line in the sand so we can stop looking back and start looking forward. This is broken into three categories:

- Own the loss
- Face the emotions
- Get closure.

# Own the loss

I bought a new car a few months ago and I absolutely love it! It was my choice to buy it and upgrade my previous car and I am very happy with the change. I'm actually a sales and marketing person's dream as I love all the bells and whistles. It's for people like me that they build all of those extra features and buttons, and we are more than happy to pay extra and get the top of the line for those fun gadgets. They often don't change anything about the way we drive but, oooh, to be able to pick the interior colour lights in my car each day … so much fun!

Okay, I digress. So, I am really happy with this change and Evie (yes, of course my car has a name) is right at home and part of the family. I tell you this because I want to emphasise that this change was 100 per cent my choice and an exciting and great change, but I still lost so many things …

The day Evie arrived and gorgeous George (yes, my previous car) was traded was a bit of a struggle. While I was gaining so much with my new car, I was also losing quite a few things, and my mind (especially my emotional mind) was struggling.

I was losing:

- the familiarity of my old car and how all the gadgets worked
- the comfort that I had created in George
- the memories and smell of George
- money out of my savings as Evie was more expensive than the trade-in price of George.

And the list goes on …

To process through this change, I had to Own It! Own the reality of the situation, but in addition, own everything that I would lose. The reality was that I was getting a shiny new car and this meant I would lose some things in the process. I had to weigh up in my head what I stood to gain vs what I stood to lose. We know this guides every decision we make, yet quite often in change we ignore what we stand to lose and just focus (or try to force people to focus) on the gain. The neural pathways that are embedded in our mind know that there will be something missing. To ignore this does not make it go away. It creates doubt and fear. Have we done the right thing? Do we really want to do this? Like any other decision in life, there comes a point where we must truly Own It and be accepting of the decision we have made. Without this ownership, the change is already doomed for failure as we are stuck at the beginning of the EI process and can't move forward.

If we look at a workplace change of getting a new leader, regardless of whether we liked, respected or got along with our previous leader, there will be a loss.

Regardless of whether the loss is good or bad, there is still a loss, and we could be losing:

- an existing bond, relationship or friendship
- the trust and feeling of safety we have with the current leader
- the feeling of knowing what to expect from them and them knowing what to expect of us.

These losses could be related to a positive and strong relationship or a negative and poor relationship. We can even lose the excuses for us not liking work or justification for our unhappiness or underperformance. For example, if we have always blamed our performance on our leader being terrible, then all of a sudden, they leave, we get a new leader and we still don't like our job.

Yes, there is a lot to gain from having a new leader too, and I am not ignoring this. But the first step is focusing purely on the loss. We are not just identifying but acknowledging and owning the loss. The gain will come in the later stages.

Imagine winning the lotto. It would be amazing, but it can create a loss of anonymity, drive and purpose in life, and change relationships with friends or family members. We could lose the financial worry that we have always had taking up space in our mind and suddenly feel lost and empty.

Going in to work with your day planned out only to find out that due to a colleague being absent, you get the amazing opportunity to step into their role for the day (which is one that you have been dreaming of doing)! This could be a great opportunity, but it also carries with it a loss of your organised day. The tasks that you had planned will no longer be done and this will impact tomorrow and the rest of the week. You may also feel a loss of being in control and knowing what you are doing.

## Ask

Think of change that has happened in your life both in and out of work and list all the losses that occurred. What changes have occurred to the people around you and what are their losses? All losses should be voiced, discussed and acknowledged.

## Face the emotions

With every moment comes an emotional response. Remember, this is where we are in our own head when we are going through the Face It step in the EI process. The difference in the change intelligence process is that Face It doesn't just happen in our own head: it becomes external as well. It's time to understand the emotions that not just we are feeling but that everyone is feeling due to the change. These could be very mixed emotions. They could be excited, relieved, nervous, betrayed, deserted, scared, lost and others. Either way, every single one of these emotions needs to be felt.

It takes time and the right environment to identify each emotion and what is driving it. This is where we always face the emotions but don't unpack our bags and stay there. It is okay to feel emotions. It is not okay to ignore them or downplay them. There is a reason the mind is creating these emotions. They are coming from something that has triggered a neural pathway in the mind and the fight-or-flight response has been activated. This requires attention. Yes, we know that our mind does a good job of overreacting at times and the situation is often not even close to what our mind is predicting, yet something is not 100 per cent right in the mind and that requires attention and processing.

The emotions that arise with change tend to be more intense given the disruption and loss in our mind. The emotions that are attached to the loss must not only be faced by us, but they must also be discussed together with the drivers of the change. We need the people who are instigating this change to be aware of the impact, the loss and how it is making us feel. We want these emotions to be acknowledged and not ignored by other people. We want them to show that while the change will bring some amazing and exciting new things, it will also create other emotions attached to the loss. So even though we have to face it in our own head, during change intelligence, Face It must be done externally, together with everyone involved.

Once the loss/es have been identified, instigate some conversations:

- 'I know there is a loss with every change. How are you feeling about what you are losing?' (or 'What are you losing with this change?')
- 'Let's take a moment to talk about what the loss is, and the emotions attached.'
- 'What can we do to help you acknowledge and process the emotions attached to the loss?'

With my new car, it was completely okay to be a bit sad for what I was losing. There were great times and great memories attached to the car. I didn't ignore this; I spoke about it with my husband and kids, and we had a few laughs at some of the stupidity that happened in it and how it was a great car, and we would miss it.

With a new leader, don't just focus on the bad part of the loss. Be thankful for the growth, the opportunities, challenges and learnings. In some cases, we learn from leaders how to be a great leader ourselves or even just a decent human being. Other times, we learn what not to do as a leader and we vow never to become that kind of leader as we know the impact it can have. There is always something to be thankful for or a conversation to be had about the loss.

The size of the change will determine the style and length of this step. If it is a small change like the change in today's work plan, a quick conversation will be all that is needed:

'Can we make this work today? How will it impact the plans you already have today? What will you lose due to this change? How do you feel about that? Do you want to talk about it in more detail?'

If the change is on a larger scale or likely to have a greater impact, a more formal conversation is recommended.

## Ask

When thinking about a recent change that has impacted you, what emotions were attached to the change and the losses? How could you instigate a conversation with people around you to support them to face and process the emotions attached to the loss?

# Get closure

To finalise the Own and Face the Loss step, some form of closure is required. This is the point where we draw a line in the sand—the finalising of what we are losing. The ability to look back and reflect before we think about moving forward.

We've felt and processed; now we ask ourselves:

- What would it take for us to be okay with this loss?

- What will create that line in the sand?

- How can we start to reflect on the loss as the past: remembering the good times, celebrating, showing gratitude with a growth mindset?

- What action is required to create this closure?

The answer to these questions is not going to be the same for everyone impacted, even if they are feeling similar emotions. Leverage the strength of the whole group to think of actions that would create closure for them and a chance to flip any fixed mindset emotions into a growth mindset. To highlight the positives, own the reality of the situation and move on with acceptance and gratitude.

Again, the size and impact of the change is going to guide this closure. I've heard some people refer to it as similar to grief and, yes, it is in a way. It's our mind processing the grief of losing something.

Gorgeous George (my old car) received a full detailing service to look even more gorgeous and I was there to hand over the keys to the new owners and mention a few times how great he was and how much I loved the car so that I felt like they were going to appreciate him. It's not a lot, but that's what was required in my head: the closure of passing the keys and watching him get driven away.

For a new leader, it's the closure of the previous leader that is required. This might be done through a reflection, a team meeting or a one-on-one meeting with the outgoing leader to reflect on time with the leader, personal growth and learnings. It might be an event, celebration or gift to recognise their last day to create closure and face the emotions that have been building and own the ending.

I heard a poor example of this recently where a client had a very impactful member of their organisation move on. The employee was well liked and had made many great, impactful changes to the organisation. Once they left the organisation, their name kind of got banished! The employees were told they were not to mention this person's name or refer to the way they had previously done their job. Any time anyone made reference to them or how they performed in their job, they were shut down and told to move on. This totally lacks closure of the loss. What would have been better is to understand and have the conversation about the benefits that came with doing it the way the previous employee had done it and how those benefits could be incorporated into some new options.

Two of my clients have moved buildings in the past 12 months. One of them did it extremely well (let's call them Company A) whereas the other move was done poorly (let's them call Company B). Both new buildings are spectacular! They have the most impressive technology, views and benefits. When the day of the move arrived, Company A asked everyone to arrive as normal to their current building.

The floor was empty, they spoke together about the memories on that floor. How they were such a small business when they first moved in and how successfully and quickly the team had grown so that they no longer fit, and how those last 12 months were a tad uncomfortable while they had desks in walkways and were very close to each other. They joked about the intimacy of the set-up at the end and how it actually brought them closer together. No-one knew at this point where the new building was. The team was then split into smaller teams of three to four and sent on an 'Amazing Race' around the city. They had riddles that needed solving, they had items to pick up for morning tea and they had to make their way to the surprise new office as a bit of a fun competition. If I stop the story there for a moment, the first step of change intelligence — Owning and Facing the Loss — was done brilliantly.

Company B engaged its staff and kept them updated in the lead-up to the move. They even offered for some people to go and do a site visit of the new office. When it came to moving day, they all packed up their belongings and left the old office to go home. The next day they turned up to the new office. By the end of the first day there was already noise overheard about the most minor things — things that were small but it was like they were looking at everything with a pessimistic, glass-half-empty approach. They were countering all of the positives with negativity due to their minds not being ready to move forward: 'It's so hard to get parking here' and 'The coffee shop downstairs makes terrible coffee'. As the days went on, there were comments like, 'The view is great but the sun reflecting off the water is so glary for my eyes.' There were some people really struggling with the change. There were also a good portion of people who loved the new office, and these people tended to be higher on the change scale while those struggling were lower. You can imagine the impact those who were struggling were having on the vibe and energy of the rest of the team.

Unfortunately, while the new change was exciting, there hadn't been any form of closure or owning/facing the loss. This is what they were struggling with. There were things that they loved about the new office and the sell for the new office was done well, but management had completely skipped steps 1 and 2 of change intelligence and jumped straight to step 3. There were things people loved at the old office that they had lost, and this was being ignored. The new office was being pushed in their faces to love and be grateful for, but their mind was still attached to the losses and really struggling.

I've heard team members in other organisations still clinging to memories and struggling after a move or merger that happened more than three years ago.

**Creating the action around the closure is pivotal, but it is also pointless if we haven't Owned It and Faced It prior to this.**

Without this, there will be people still stuck in the past looping in their own head and fighting to not let go of the past regardless of how good the new future is.

## Ask

What closure is lacking from your life, your team, your workplace, your family and your friends? What past are you still holding onto? What will you do to create the closure?

Step 1 involves a lot of mind work and leverages our EI in every aspect. Some have drawn comparisons to the grief cycle and while changes in our workplace don't compare to grief, the process our mind goes through is very similar. Regardless of the size of the loss, we need to Own It, face the emotions and get closure.

# Chapter reflection

- Step 1 of the change intelligence process has three components: own the loss, face the emotions and get closure.

- The loss needs acknowledgement and to be voiced. Even the most amazing changes will always have a loss that needs to be recognised so the mind can go through the process of losing something before it sees the gains.

- To process emotions, we face each emotion to understand where it has come from and what is driving it. This is not just our personal emotions but the emotions that others are feeling. Instigate conversations to help the process.

- Closure requires some form of action. Something that draws a line in the sand and acknowledges the past before looking forward to the future. Sometimes it will need to be a significant gesture and other times, a simple conversation.

- Reflecting on step 1, identify an upcoming change and how you will implement the key areas to help your mind own and face the loss.

# Chapter 7

# STEP 2: FEEL AND ASK THROUGH THE LIMINAL SPACE

Step 2 is when we progress from the 'old world' closure but are not yet ready for the 'new world' change — it's the liminal space.

The liminal space refers to the area between one point and the next point — like the space between worlds. In other words, when you know you have moved on from one point, but you are not quite at the next point. It can feel like a real void in our head. It can even cause exhaustion from the previous stage, resulting in a low care factor or sensory overload.

This is when we just need space. Space to not make any big decisions or use our brain in a new or learning capacity. We want to disengage our emotional mind as much as possible and just let the conscious and logical mind do what it does to get through the day. We don't want to know about the shiny new toy right now and we don't want to get excited; we just want to *be*.

In this chapter we get teams involved and engaged in what is coming and provide the support and direction they each need to move forward. This space can create the need for some tough and emotionally driven conversations so effective communication is a key focus, along with honest transparency. Feeling and asking through the liminal space is broken into three areas:

- Provide support and direction
- Communicate effectively
- Ensure ongoing transparency.

## Providing support and direction

Our ability to Feel It and tap into our leadership skills is a priority at this stage. With an emotional flatness among the team as they transition through the liminal space they really don't want to hear about the future just yet nor do they want to be forced to do anything. Spend time sitting in the current state with the team leveraging empathy. Remember that empathy is not putting ourselves in their shoes: they're not your shoes, so stay out of them! We are putting ourselves into their emotional state. The situation becomes irrelevant. There is no space for judgement or 'What would I do?' Recognise the emotion they are feeling and recall when the last time was you felt that emotion.

What is the *worst* thing that someone could say or do to you when you felt that emotion? Skip that! Focus on the *best* thing that someone could say or do when you were feeling that emotion.

Recognise what they need from us as leaders and the different ways they are wired.

## A great leader adapts their style to the person and situational needs in front of them.

As leaders, we offer our support and seek to understand what it will take for our team to move through this stage. Provide options or suggestions while leading by example. How we react and handle this stage will be closely watched. Our engagement, emotional intelligence and buy-in to the change will deeply influence those around us.

Look for moments to start to plant the seeds. Whether it is curiosity or inspiration, it should be small and subtle, but still be evident and not hidden. It is a gentle, slower approach and a great time to offer small areas of empowerment to both start the progress and build involvement. Ask them what the future and the change should look like. What are their ideas and how involved do they want to be? This stage overlaps some of step 1 depending on the situation, the people involved and the size of the change.

My new car, Evie, took time to adjust to. I loved the look and idea of having a new car, but there was so much I didn't know and was yet to learn. While the liminal space wasn't a big chunk of time, it did require time to understand how she actually worked and what was different from my old car, George. Launching straight into driving her without understanding the settings and buttons created confusion and frustration. I took the time to just sit in her, download the online app and set up my profile. I pushed all the buttons and went down a rabbit hole to see every option that sat behind each button. The car salesman called me after having her for 24 hours to ask if I had any questions and to find out how I was doing. This was him providing support and direction. He gave me his mobile to call if I had anything further but still rang me again after a week to check in.

Having an existing leader depart and a new one start will naturally involve a liminal space while the new leader needs time to learn the ropes and get their head around the new team, environment and workplace. During this period, it would be naïve to expect the team to jump straight from losing their old leader to loving their new one. They likely don't know them so it will take observations, conversations and experiences for them to create the emotional connection, whether it be good or bad. Some people will do this quite quickly, while for others it will take time. Either way, it is about providing support and direction while they go through it and not forcing them to jump open armed into a new relationship with a new leader they don't know. Answer the questions, tread carefully and be slowly guided by their needs. Relationships can't be forced.

Company A had created the perfect liminal space while the team were on their Amazing Race. The leaders had provided the team with hints and clues to solve that were seeds being planted for the new building. They gave them time in the in-between (liminal) space to build fresh emotions and memories to attach to the new building. This was so much better than walking them straight there because they would have done step 1 well but skipped step 2.

## Ask

What support and direction does your team currently need? How are you using empathy to provide this in a way that helps them through the void and plants seeds for the future?

# Communicating effectively

Communication through this stage can be led by emotions rather than our logical brain. This means that some communications will be difficult and challenging to have. Whether emotions are at a high or at a very low level, ensure your emotions as a leader are always under control. Don't over-plan the conversation and avoid being defensive or feeling that justification is necessary. This is your opportunity to apply all of your EI skills, remembering the emotional undertone of the words we use. Help the other person involved in the communication to Ask It and smash through fear, doubt and indecisiveness. They should own the outcomes and actions. Continue to communicate throughout and reflect after each communication.

Engaging in difficult conversations is no small feat. For this reason, part IV of this book is dedicated to them. This will help build your communication skills and toolkit for difficult conversations before entering a conversation.

The first difficult conversation I had about Evie was with myself. With lots of gadgets came lots of beeping from the car. It was about understanding the beeping but also adjusting the settings to get the balance right between the features, providing me with the safety that I needed (as I'm a pretty average driver, so the more safety features the better) and not letting the car actually take over the driving. The toughest conversation was the one (and ongoing one) that I have with my husband Mark. He is definitely not a gadget, beeping or self-driving car kind of person. His frustrations with my beautiful new Evie were annoying not just for him but for me because I had to listen to them every time he was driving. Knowing that my husband's relationship with change is much lower on the scale to mine, I had to get out of my own head and appreciate how much change was involved for him — and it wasn't just about the new car; it was about the level of change.

**With the team and the new leader in the liminal space, we can end up butting heads when we are driven by our emotional brain rather than our logical brain.**

This will result in some tough conversations. These conversations might be around expectations, performance or practically any area. A change in people and culture will always test existing boundaries along with new boundaries that need to be created. They might have been triggered around fear of change, fear of judgement or misjudging people's intentions. Regardless of the cause, ownership of the reality of the situation and a difficult conversation is required. Don't ignore the problem.

## Ask

What conversations have you been avoiding? How will you approach these conversations within the next 48 hours?

If you are like many adults and avoid difficult conversations, enjoy diving deep into part IV, where I dissect and teach you how to have efficient difficult conversations.

# Ensuring ongoing transparency

In the liminal space, our mind is feeling the void, and towards the end will start looking for answers or guidance. The fear of the unknown, next steps or even the fear of losing control will see us relying on trust to help us through. Honesty and transparency are some of the core drivers of trust, and being open and sharing the intentions will help to build this trust. Without trust, progressing to the next stage is an absolute waste of time. Never risk misinformation or purposely withhold information, especially when it is evident that you are withholding information. Trust is a hard emotion to build and even harder if the trust has been lost or damaged. Trust is covered in more detail in chapter 16.

Communications should be regular and ongoing and should be a mix of both formal and informal, scheduled and ad hoc. Create the right balance as too much communication can also make people switch off, and no-one is begging to be inundated with multiple emails in their inbox. The communications need purpose, to be clear and precise and cover all four modalities of the people in your team:

- visual
- kinaesthetic
- digital
- auditory.

What I mean by this is that we know everyone utilises all four of these modalities when communicating, but all of us have a default that we align with more frequently.

Visual people want to see it and observe what happens and how it looks. Communication should include infographics, diagrams, the big picture, colour and images.

Kinaesthetic people want to use their hands and connect with the person, the information and to get involved. Is there something they can test out or touch? Communications should be in person and should create an emotional connection.

Digital people want the details — the full details. So, communication will require the research, the data, the manual, something that they can read to understand every step. They will also ask quite a few questions until they have everything they need.

Auditory people will want to talk it through, not in a loud or large group but in their own space and led by their questions to process the information through repetition in conversation and clarification. If we are unsure what default modality the person is, ask them how they prefer to receive communication. If it is a group of people, cover all four default modalities.

Own It and call out any errors or unexpected results due to the change along the way. We tend to have a habit in the workplace of everything needing to work out and for us to be right and successful. This can at times cause us to hide or downplay things when they don't go to plan. We put blinkers on and just keep going for the end prize knowing perfectly well that it's unlikely but not wanting to admit an error, unsuccessful outcome or failure. As we know, even the best laid plans don't work out. It is key to be transparent. If the amazing change was expected to do X but only delivers a small part of Y, don't try to hide this. Call it out and be transparent in saying that while the aim was X, here is the reality and this is why we have landed here. Sometimes, when things really aren't going to plan, it might be best to abort the change. This takes huge awareness and ownership, yet often our fear of failure means we push forward and implement something that is really substandard and quickly walk away while others are left to deal with the aftermath. Remember that EI isn't about getting it right every time; it's about having the self-awareness and ownership to admit it when it doesn't work and to do what is required to make it right.

Like any form of change, there were some things that I didn't love about Evie. Yes, they were minor, but they existed. I spoke to the car salesman to find out why, even after I supposedly permanently turned off one of the beeping features, I had to turn it off every time I started the car as it didn't default to off. Also, being a bit of a 'Karen', I mentioned that the reversing auto collision braking was too sensitive to my shrubs and trees when I reversed out of my garage. His honesty and transparency were perfect. He agreed that the car not saving the switching off feature was super annoying; they had raised it with the car maker and will continue to at their meetings until it is fixed. At the same time, he was able to give me a great workaround to make it so much easier to switch off. As for my 'Karen' moment, he paused and calmly yet subtly called me out on my shit! 'Amy, that's what it is supposed to do. Maybe don't reverse into your shrubs and trees and it won't go off.' Point taken, ha ha! I reiterate: I'm really not the world's best driver.

The new leader will always differ from the old leader. That's the great thing about people having different wiring: we have slightly different approaches and with that comes learning opportunities and sometimes annoyance! The worst thing the new leader can do is to come straight in and start making changes, comments or judgements, or expecting the team to buy in to them and everything they say. The team should also take some time to let the leader settle in and for them to get to know the new leader and how they work and are wired.

For most of us, when we start a new leadership position, there are several emotions challenging us, such as nerves, imposter syndrome, fear of not being liked or being judged, lack of understanding, and wanting to prove ourselves to others or even more to ourselves for our own confidence. A new leader should take time in their liminal space to understand all aspects of the new role and to settle in. During this period, they should be transparent with everyone about what their approach is and — even more importantly — to share some of their 90-day plan (their actions for the first 90 days in the role) so the team knows what to expect. Without information, our fight or flight can kick in and members of the team will go into emotional hijacks causing defensive mechanisms and pushback to the new leader.

## Ask

How would you currently rate your transparency with your team? Is there a way that you can improve transparency to create more comfort and trust within your team?

Remember to implement the small, incremental, transparent planting of seeds during this time. Don't hold back: people will respect you so much more when you are transparent.

# Chapter reflection

- Traversing the liminal space takes time and involvement. We can't expect people to go straight from the past to the future; we need time to just 'be'. This is where providing support and direction, communicating effectively and being transparent helps this void to have meaning.

- Providing support and direction looks different for each person and each change. Empathy is the key skill to understanding the emotion and what is needed based on the emotion, not the situation.

- When emotions are high, effective communication becomes number one. Don't overplan and be guided by empathy and the emotions of the conversation.

- Always be transparent! As soon as people can see there is something either not going to plan or details not being provided, defence mechanisms will kick in. It's a given that things won't always go the way we hoped. Be transparent and communicate in a way people understand.

- Reflecting on step 2, are you providing the time and support for your teams to be in the liminal space? Is the communication effective and transparent? What can you do as a leader to improve the liminal space for your team and the outcome of the change?

## Chapter 8

# STEP 3: DRIVE THE CHANGE LIKE A CHAMPION

The time has finally arrived to sell the change! I'll now introduce Step 3: The Change. For our EI it's about leveraging our motivation and drive.

This is the step that most leaders usually nail when it comes to change. They do tend to jump straight to this step, missing the first two steps, which results in a lack of buy-in and success in the change. Company B did this well by planning, involving and engaging the team with the new building but without the first two steps, it didn't have the desired outcome.

In this chapter we break down step 3, which is all about launching and implementing the new change successfully.

This requires details and plans — and while we are heavily focused on the process, we never forget the people. Drive the change like a champion is broken down into three areas:

- Have a project plan
- Put people before process
- Involve and engage.

# Have a project plan

It still shocks me how many workplaces roll out major change without a project plan. Every project, regardless of the size, requires a plan. It's not so much for the actual project outcome; it's for the process of driving the change. It doesn't always need to be a massive 20-page project document with endless appendices and attachments. It can be as simple as having a documented who, what, when, how and why. We need to be extremely clear on the purpose and steps of the implementation. Ask for a copy of the project plan and if there isn't one, create a basic guide for yourself so you are prepared with questions at the implementation stage. The EI process is also a great way to lay out the project plan and ensure you have EI covered at the same time. You can use the questions in figure 8.1 to create the plan.

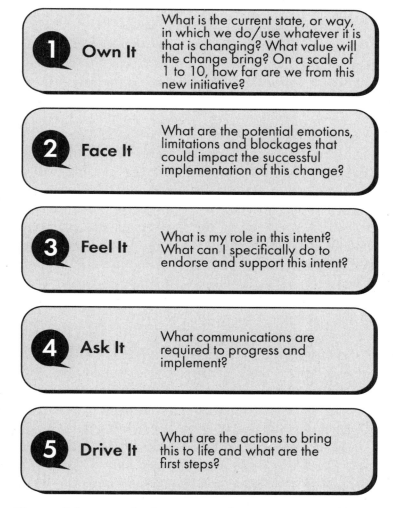

**Figure 8.1:** using the EI process to lay out a project plan.

## Own It

*What is the current state, or way, in which we do/use whatever it is that is changing? What value will the change bring? On a scale of 1 to 10, how far are we from this new initiative?*

When purchasing my new car, the current state was that my existing car, George, was clocking up a lot of kilometres. The value was depreciating and as the car gets older, there is a higher risk of needing major repairs. Buying a new car will provide a reset on kilometres; it will have the latest car technology, decrease the risk of major repairs and therefore increase the value. We were at a 6 out of 10 on the scale for the new initiative as I knew exactly what car I wanted, I had the finance and I knew the dealer I was purchasing it from. It was just a matter of ordering the car and processing the paperwork.

Let's look at another common change in the workplace, a change in leadership. The current state is that the existing leader is leaving the company for a complete change in career. The value is the opportunity to give the team a fresh leader with a slightly different style of leadership to inspire and motivate the team in different ways. So, on a scale of 1 to 10 as to where the new initiative is currently at, it would be a 3 out of 10. The couple of potential internal candidates is a start but there is still a lot left to do including engaging an external recruiter, advertising/searching, conducting interviews, recruiting and onboarding to make progress on this change initiative.

## *Face It*

*What are the potential emotions, limitations and blockages that could impact the successful implementation of this change?*

With my car, it included frustration if the car takes ages to arrive, worry if I can't get the trade-in I want for my old car, concern if I don't like the new car, limitations if the car is not available or doesn't have the optional extras I want and blockages if my finance falls through. All these emotions needed to be faced and mitigated. To do that, I asked myself 'if this does happen, what will I do then?' By asking the question, I am facing the emotion, and finding a solution to every potential emotional concern helps to process the emotion and move forward with the prepared solution regardless of whether it happens or not.

With a new leader, concern and disruption to a team and their performance threatens, along with possible dislike or anger towards the new leader and fear within the new leader. Add to that the limitations of not giving the new leader a chance and making a biased judgement and potential blockages of shutting down and refusing to be a decent team member, or the new leader not being the right person for the role. These are all very possible in a workplace environment and can become the elephant in the room if we ignore them. Identify all the risks and mixed emotions, identify the best way to approach them; then be aware if they do occur as they should be immediately addressed.

## *Feel It*

*What is my role in this intent? What can I specifically do to endorse and support this intent?*

My role was the lead role in purchasing my new car, Evie. To endorse and support this intent, I was responsible for all actions and decision-making, from doing the paperwork to transferring payment, to trading in my old car.

The role for people involved with a new leader differs from one person to another. If I was the person this new leader would be reporting to, I am responsible for choosing the right candidate, supporting the team through the process and ensuring the success of the new leader in the role to meet expectations. If I was a member of the team, my role would be to create a new relationship with the leader, understand expectations and help them to understand the current state of the team.

## *Ask It*

*What communications are required to progress and implement?*

My husband was my main communication to ensure we were on the same page. Also to form a relationship with the car dealer so that the process was smooth, and expectations were met for both parties.

When there is a new leader, a communication plan should be developed. This should include what communications will be going out, when they will go out, why it's important for each one to happen, who will be responsible for making it happen and how the communication will be delivered (platform).

## Drive It

*What are the actions to bring this to life and what are the first steps?*

Research the new car, its features and pricing. Make an appointment with the car dealer to chat and test drive the car.

Work with HR to develop a clear job description for the new leader as well as a recruitment process including who will be involved in the process, what stakeholders will be impacted and why, what the ideal candidate looks like, logistics around timing and resources, and the actual step-by-step process. Help to develop a plan for the first 90 days and determine how to induct the new recruit into the organisation.

All project plans should be 100 per cent transparent and made available. Anything withheld can sabotage the acceptance of the change. If it is not made available, people will naturally go to worst-case scenario in their heads. Of course, not everything goes to plan, so this plan should not be set in stone. It is more of a guide. Be honest and transparent and be ready to revise, update or change it based on the situation and progression.

As the plan progresses, provide updates on wins, even the small ones. This creates a release of the chemical dopamine within our brain and is used to leverage the motivation. The easiest way to trigger the release of dopamine in our brain is to break down the steps into smaller tasks. As each task is completed, we feel accomplishment and this helps to create dopamine. Share the updates to show progress.

Whether the plan is a 15-minute brain dump on a notepad, a detailed conversation in a meeting or an impressive digital interactive plan, it creates clarity and drive in our mind and in the minds of everyone involved in supporting the implementation of the change.

## Ask

Have you seen the project plan for any upcoming changes? Is there an opportunity to create even a simple project plan for a change that you have coming up?

# Put people before process

The response and progress that people make should always trump the project plan. Don't get so attached to the project plan that it becomes the law and regardless of how people are responding just stick straight to your schedule. We can have the best laid plans, but people are complex creatures! We make plans based on assumptions of how we think they will work and what we think people require from us. We don't always get these assumptions right. Read the room! Be aware and observant of how people are coping. Identify what stage of the EI process each person is at and what they require to move forward to the next stage.

## Ask

Are they looping in their own head and have they not faced their emotions completely? Are they digging their head in the sand and not owning the reality of the situation? Has something been identified in the Feel It stage that wasn't considered and will make a big impact that requires risk mitigation before proceeding?

If any of these questions mean the change needs to pause or the project plan requires alterations, then do it! The people are far more important than the process. Without the people, the process is completely irrelevant.

We know that our mind leads everything that we do and for every decision we make there is that weigh-up in our mind asking, 'What do I stand to gain vs what do I stand to lose?' This is where understanding the different personalities in change and taking the best leader approach pays off. Provide the support that is required at all stages.

It would be unrealistic to think that every change will get 100 per cent agreeance or buy-in. This isn't about striving for agreeance. They don't need to agree, but they do need to accept. The standard 80/20 rule comes into play where we aim for 80 per cent onboard before moving on. We will continue to work closely with the other 20 per cent as the change progresses.

To Drive It, together we set team goals and expectations that are realistic. Reflect regularly and check in on mindset. Identify ways to better support mindset and lift people to the highest potential.

When buying a new car, even though there is plenty of value in the structure and usability of the car, ultimately, we must be happy with it and like it. This is putting the people before the process. It won't matter how good the car is — the value, the kilometres — if we don't actually like it. If we don't like it, we will always find other things wrong with it and reasons why we don't like it. The acceptance will never happen, the decision will take up real estate in our mind and we will be thinking about how we can get a new car again, rejecting the success of this change.

Losing a leader and recruiting the right new leader is super important. But more important is retaining the team of people around them so we don't find ourselves not just recruiting a new leader but also a new team.

> **A leader is only successful if their team are successful and true success is reliant on happiness.**

So, listen to the team, put the people first and make sure it's a good fit to achieve the end result.

## Ask

Can you think of times where either the process was put before the people or when people have halted a project due to its impact? What was the outcome of the situation?

# Involve and engage

We naturally care more about things that we have an emotional connection with. Anything that has caused us to think and respond with an emotion creates a form of memory in our mind and therefore an emotional connection. Get your team as involved as possible. Certainly, don't force it upon them but have a chat to find out how involved they want to be. We can also involve people without them having to do anything by simply keeping them in the loop or asking for their thoughts, ideas or feedback.

Monitor the engagement, not just by what people are saying, but what people are doing. Address any concerns as they arise and continue to check in on their engagement throughout this stage.

Most importantly, create a celebration, some excitement around the shiny new toy. Something for people to look forward to or feel hopeful about. The less it looks like a process and the more connection and drive the change has, the greater the chance of a successful implementation and outcome.

The inaugural drive in Evie was first with my son, Koen, and his girlfriend while they tested out every feature, connected their phones and music and had their own new car celebration. Our daughter, Amelia, created what felt like a dance party including a light show during her first drive and my husband created his own profile, got all his settings locked in and went for a drive.

A new leader will naturally impact the culture. Hit this full on with a celebration. Create some type of welcome for the new leader, a chance for the team to bond and get to know each other. Let them decide what this looks like. Support them to find their synergies and opportunities. Have some fun!

## Ask

How are you involving and engaging the people in your team? How involved does each person want to be? How can you create engagement for those who want little involvement?

# This is exhausting!

Using examples like buying a new car or a new leader starting in a team can help to understand change intelligence, but by this stage it can also feel exhausting! You might be wondering 'Does she really expect us to do this process with every bit of change? How does this relate to day-to-day workings in my team?'

Like EI, especially empathy, change intelligence is exhausting to do every single time any form of change occurs. I mean, change is happening daily and even several times a day. It is not imperative that this change intelligence happens at this level of detail every time. If you don't use it, your change won't always fail. But like every aspect of EI, when you do choose to use it, the outcome is always going to be better than when you don't. Also, like EI, you can go through this change intelligence process in a 15-minute conversation, or you can conduct it over a six-month period — it all depends on the size and impact of the change.

If it is a simple, small change to an action plan or how you had previously agreed to do something, then a conversation could be enough. As a team, own that the change is happening and identify together what the loss is. Feel and ask your way through the liminal space right there in that conversation, providing support. Ask how the team feels about the change, answer questions or concerns, be transparent and then drive the new change by highlighting the plan and next steps. Read the people for buy-in and identify ways to involve and engage the team where appropriate. This can easily be done in 15 minutes or even less.

## Ask

What change is upcoming or happening right now in your workplace? How can you use the change intelligence process to be better prepared and to deliver the change with successful implementation and acceptance from your people?

If the change is a medium-sized change such as altering the steps to an existing process, changes to a product or service offering or a new update to a well-known system, then a one-hour meeting or several small workshops may be required to go into the change intelligence process in more detail.

When the change is large or of decent impact — such as a restructure, reform, merger or acquisition — I would always recommend change intelligence. In this instance it is not just required, but a must for true success and buy-in.

## Chapter reflection

- Step 3 is where we naturally want to be. To implement the change successfully, there needs to be a plan and the people should remain key. Involvement and engagement across the teams will bring the change to life.

- Be prepared with a plan to drive the change. Even if it's simple, people will want to know the 'next steps' and the 'how' of what is coming. Remember, always people before process.

- Be realistic: change comes in all sizes. Adapt your approach to the size of the change and the reaction from the people impacted.

- Reflecting on step 3, how well are you doing this? Are you expecting the change to speak for itself or how are you really driving it with details, people and engagement?

# Part III

# DIFFICULT CONVERSATIONS

Difficult conversations are most often avoided by leaders. They are not something that any human being really enjoys. I would be concerned if I met someone who loved having a difficult conversation — that would be a little weird! A difficult conversation is any interaction with another person that is likely to cause unexpected and/or unenjoyable emotions from either of the people involved. This is why we struggle with difficult conversations: we fear not knowing how the situation will pan out, how the other person will react or how well we will manage our emotions during the conversation.

Difficult conversations in the workplace can be triggered by a number of things, with some of the most common being that the team member:

- has continually been late to work
- is underperforming
- is accused of making unacceptable remarks to other team members
- is disconcerted because their role has been made redundant
- has a hygiene issue that is impacting many people (yes, sadly this happens — the leader's role can be so much fun!).

It is the difficult conversations that reaffirm to us that success in a role is so much more than the technical aspect: it's every part of the human interaction. It's how well we communicate, work together and create an environment that has balance. It's the leader's role to create and maintain this balance.

We also simply like to be liked. As socially interactive creatures, it's nice to get along with people and to feel like other people like us. What if the difficult conversation leads to the person not liking us or when other people hear about it, they decide they don't like us. Being liked is equivalent to an affirmation that we are part of society and doing well as a human being. I'm not saying that this is true. I'm simply saying that society and the wiring of our minds can have us thinking this. So, the risk of upsetting this feeling or relationship is not one that we will happily leap towards, whether it is in the workplace or in any other area of our life.

The easiest option, and the road of least resistance, is to simply avoid the conversation altogether. Stick our head in the sand and pretend it's not happening or convince ourselves that it's not that bad and it will, or is already, improving by itself. Sure, there may be some situations where this holds true and the situation does improve. If this is the case, thank your lucky stars as it's a rare occurrence — but don't celebrate too quickly because there's sure to be a new situation not far around the corner requiring a difficult conversation.

In part III, I will:

- challenge your excuse mindset and identify the impact it is having on your actions

- introduce five easy steps as a guide for navigating difficult conversations, including the hugely important step of not over-preparing

- identify the impact that emotions have in our conversations and how to follow the emotion and not the situation

- put all the skills into practice with five of the most common reasons for difficult conversations

- develop your communication skills in managing up

- ensure that growth and learnings are actually happening through reflection.

I'm pumped to share with you my tools for dealing with difficult conversations to achieve positive outcomes and progress. Let's get into it!

# Chapter 9

# THE EXCUSE MINDSET

Our mind really is our closest friend. Sometimes it's our best friend and sometimes it's quite the opposite. When a difficult conversation rears its ugly head, it's the excuse mindset that has our back. It not only helps us to avoid and not make it happen, but it also justifies and helps us to feel okay about not doing it. As though it's not our fault — it's totally out of our hands. It's so much easier when we aren't the reason for something not happening; it takes the personal side out of it and also removes accountability. We use this excuse mindset to make ourselves feel better about not acting. The excuse mindset can be activated at any time, not just when a difficult conversation is required, but any time we don't want to do something.

This chapter might really challenge your mindset and beliefs. We live in a world where these excuses are not only acceptable but also frequently endorsed. We are all guilty of using them at different times. As you read through the chapter, keep an open mind. Using these excuses doesn't make you a bad person. The purpose of this chapter is to flip our mindset and take ownership when we choose not to do something rather than blaming something or someone else.

There are three main areas to our excuse mindset: limitations, fears and time. Let's start with limitations.

## Limitations

The conversations that happen between our conscious and our subconscious mind draw from different parts of our brain. Our conscious mind uses more of our logical and analytical brain, whereas our subconscious uses our emotional brain, values, beliefs and experiences. Sometimes these areas do not quite align. Our logical brain knows what to do but our subconscious mind is not quite on board with it. This creates a limitation in our ability to move forward. It doesn't feel right. It might make us feel a bit nervous or sick in the stomach. The emotions that are being produced by our emotional brain are limiting the logical brain from taking full control. Imagine working with someone who is also a friend, and their performance is not where it should be. The logical part of our brain knows that this is not good and that it's our role as a leader to address this on behalf of the organisation, the team and everyone involved. But the emotional brain is thinking about the friendship and potential impacts of having this difficult conversation. Our emotions start to kick in and create a limitation between our conscious and subconscious mind. Hello avoidance!

Cognitive dissonance takes it one step further. This is when we have a strong value or belief in place, yet our actions are doing the opposite. I might strongly believe that living my very best life means feeding my body with nutritional food, drinking plenty of water and doing regular exercise and that this will result in me living a long and healthy life. Yet, I don't do regular exercise and have a love obsession with sugar and carbs. This is a cognitive dissonance. I might strongly believe the workplace I am in is toxic and the way that I am treated is not healthy or acceptable, yet I choose to get up every morning and go to work there rather than addressing the issues, which actually endorses the behaviours by continuing to let them happen. This is a cognitive dissonance where our values/beliefs and actions are misaligned causing limitations in our mind.

The easiest way, or the path of least resistance, is generally what we look for in the first instance in any situation. When this is not straightforward or available, we create limitations or even convince ourselves it is impossible to do simply because it's not easy. If one of our systems at work is not capable of doing something, we are quick to say it can't be done before considering whether there is a manual way or a workaround that would achieve a similar result. This means more and/or harder work for us — creating a limitation — so we avoid it all together.

We might have a team member who is working remotely and only comes in to the workplace once a month. We have received several complaints over the past few days from customers about this team member. They were in the workplace last week so they are not due to come in again for another three weeks. The issue wouldn't be easy to address over the phone or using technology and we don't want to ask them to come into the office, so we just send through a quick email to everyone in the team reminding them of how customers should be treated hoping this team member will get the message, rather than having the difficult conversation with that person. It's the easiest path.

Justification always helps us to feel better. 'It's not my fault — it is what it is. I'm not doing this through choice — there just isn't any other option.' We are pretty good at coming up with these justifications to convince ourselves that what we are doing is right.

'My boss asked me to focus on a project this week so I can't deal with this confrontation between two team members. It will have to wait; I am needed elsewhere.'

Or, 'I had a difficult conversation with a colleague, and they cried because I shouted at them, but they are the one who did the wrong thing to start with. If they hadn't done it, then I wouldn't have had to shout at them.' Justification gives us reasons for not doing things, but it also gives us reasons for doing them poorly.

Blockers are a higher level of justification. This is when we claim we are being blocked from doing something.

'My team don't understand and are not on board with our new values because HR (human resources) didn't roll them out through the layers correctly. They did it well at management and leader level, but it didn't cascade — that's why my team aren't familiar and on board. It's not up to me as the leader to cascade it well to my team; that's on HR.' Absolutely passing the blame and labelling them as blockers! 'I don't hold regular team meetings because there isn't a room big enough on our floor to hold all my team. I am happy to do the team meetings but it's not having a big enough room that is stopping me from doing it. There is a blocker in the way, and it's not me.'

Regardless of the type of limitation occurring, these are all excuses! We are choosing to place the limitation there so we don't have to do something. It's time for us to wake up to the limitations, take true ownership and, whether we like it or not, own that the outcome is our choice — not anyone's or anything's fault.

## Ask

What limitations are forming in your excuse mindset? What are you guilty of using to avoid a difficult conversation or doing something that should be done? When will you take ownership and action?

## Fears

We know that fear is not a bad thing. Fear has a very relevant role to play within each of us and that is to keep us safe and out of any potential danger. If we look back to the early ages, this fear was extremely important to stop us from being eaten by a wild animal or getting seriously injured. These days, our environment has rapidly progressed and while we are unlikely to be at regular risk of being eaten or injured, fear finds other ways to make us feel like we need protection. These fears include:

- fear of death
- fear of loss of control
- fear of judgement
- fear of the unknown
- fear of failure.

There are many different things each of us can list as fearing, such as heights, spiders, public speaking, confined spaces, snakes, fire and birds. When it comes to fear, it's the potential/worst-case outcome that we fear more than the actual situation. So, with heights, it would be a fall resulting in death (which is really a core fear of death). Public speaking worst-case scenario tends to be being laughed at or made fun of, or not being able to answer a question, so it's a fear of judgement, failure or the unknown. When we can work out what the core fear is, we start to see it popping up in different aspects of our lives and if we can work on that core fear, we can progress in so many areas of our lives.

**When our excuse mindset kicks in, triggered by a core fear, it's our relationship with that core fear that stops us from doing whatever we should be doing.**

Our protection mechanism from the fear leads us to create the limitations mentioned earlier, and we loop around and around from excuse to fear, to excuse to fear, putting off or shutting down the required action.

Understand and take control of the core fear so that the limitation is not triggered in the first place.

## Ask

What is ultimately stopping me from doing this? What is the potential outcome that I struggle with the most should it happen? What will I do if this does happen?

# Time

Time is our number one excuse and totally lacks ownership of any kind: 'I don't/didn't have time'. It takes a mindset shift to really understand this excuse mindset as we have embedded it so deeply and it's so common in our language.

We know that we all have 24 hours in each day. None of us has any more or any less time. Time is a fundamentally international concept. It doesn't differ, no matter where you live, who you are or what you have going on. Each and every one of us has 24 hours in a day. Within this 24-hour period there are people who do absolutely extraordinary things and others who do very little. Some days we are super productive while on others we relax. Regardless of how we spend those 24 hours, it's a choice based on our priorities and potential consequences. We choose how that time is spent, and this is what we need to open our minds to and own. It's not time's fault that we didn't do it. It clearly wasn't a priority for us, and we chose to spend the time doing something else. Something of greater priority to us.

When we break down time, the context becomes so relevant. Simply looking at what happens in one minute across the world is quite staggering. I love the website *OMNI calculator*, where you can see the number of things that occur within the timespan of a minute — for example, 258 babies are born and 108 people die every minute. This is a reality check for our ever-growing world. Every minute, 203 472 222 emails are sent. Just process that: more than 203 million emails are sent every minute! If emails are the bane of your existence and you feel like you spend your workday stuck in your email inbox, this is why.

My family is a big sport-watching family and our son plays a lot of basketball. When there is a minute to go in a soccer or rugby league game, I'm pretty confident that the game is done and the score is unlikely to change. When we are watching basketball and there is one minute to go, it is still anyone's game, and the score can change dramatically.

A minute doesn't seem like much when we are sitting watching television or scrolling on our phone, yet a minute feels huge when we've just missed our train, plane or bus. Time is all about context. There are plenty of ways to use our time more efficiently; it simply comes down to our priorities. Challenge yourself for the next two weeks to look at your priorities and how you choose to spend your time. Ask yourself why what you are choosing to do is a priority over the other things on your list. Be comfortable with owning that priority and that the things you are not choosing to do are not as high a priority to you as what you are doing. It's okay that they are not a priority and that you are not doing them, but it's not time's fault. Stop blaming time and take ownership!

Before we make any decision in life, our mind weighs up: what do we stand to gain vs what do we stand to lose? The answer to this question guides the level of priority attached to what we need or want to do and therefore the likelihood of it being done. It's a great idea to even sort to-do lists into 'must-do', 'want to-do' and 'nice to-do' based on what we stand to gain vs lose. To-do lists are a fantastic way to help trigger the chemical dopamine in our brain that generates motivation, but to-do lists shouldn't start fresh every day. They should be a flowing carry-on from the day before as it is unrealistic to think that we can do absolutely everything on our list every single day. Don't set yourself up for failure — be realistic and prioritise the to-do list based on value gain. Values matrices are also a great tool to prioritise ideas and actions. A values matrix is a standard grid-based diagram with time complexity on one axis vs business value on the other. We plot each idea or action onto the grid based on the axis, as you can see in figure 9.1.

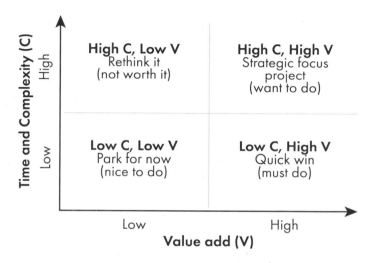

**Figure 9.1:** values matrix — a prioritisation tool

It really comes down to what we are willing to do. How hard are we willing to work? How badly do we want this done and do we really want to achieve the outcomes?

I know it can be a real struggle to accept and own that a lack of time is not a real reason but more of a bullshit excuse. Time is real. Blaming time is a bullshit excuse. Choose your time more wisely based on those things that really matter to you. If it doesn't really matter or is not a priority, own and accept that it's not a priority compared to the other ways you can spend your time. If I am asked to do something, I immediately weigh up the gain vs loss in my head and provide a realistic time frame base on priority. It's okay to say, 'My focus for today is already on other priorities but I will have an answer for you tomorrow. Does that work for you?'

If you truly think you don't have time, go into the settings in your phone and have a look at what your average time spent on social media is for one day. It's always a scary reality check for me ... aargh!

## Ask

When have you been using the excuse of a lack of time? What difficult conversations have been avoided due to 'lack of time'? Why is it not a priority for you right now? What do you stand to gain vs lose if you do or don't do something?

When you own that it's on you and not on time, priorities tend to change.

# Chapter reflection

- The excuse mindset makes us think it is okay not to do or act on something.

- The three main areas of our excuse mindset are limitations, fear and time. When we use these excuses, we completely lack ownership.

- Limitations occur between our conscious and subconscious mind and create justifiable reasons why we can't do what we should be doing. Identify these limitations and ways to mitigate them.

- When our core fears are triggered, they provide reasons to stop us from moving forward. We use these fears to justify not progressing. Addressing the core fear helps us to release the excuse mindset.

- Time is the biggest excuse we use. There is no lack of time. We all have 24 hours in a day. There is time to do it; it's our priorities that determine whether it will be done. Using time as an excuse totally lacks ownership!

- On reflection of the excuse mindset, what excuses are you using to justify not getting things done? What difficult conversations are you avoiding and when will you own them and have the conversation?

# Chapter 10

# FIVE EASY STEPS

Now that we have removed any excuses as to why we won't be having that much-needed difficult conversation, it's time to prepare for the conversation. Before we get into the actual steps of the conversation, let's talk about preparation! Our preparation is just as crucial as having the conversation, and will influence the success.

Accepting and committing to the conversation doesn't mean that, suddenly, we are comfortable and pumped about having the conversation. There is still that dread or dislike in our head. When we are feeling these emotions, our amygdala (emotional brain) is quite often triggered and this leads to an emotional hijack where our emotional brain rather than our logical brain is driving and fight or flight kicks in. Fight or flight is the survival instinct that asks us are we staying to fight or are we getting out of here in flight mode? We have already done the hard work about excuses, and 'flight' has been removed as an option from the conversation, which means our emotional mind often becomes a 'fight' mindset.

With a 'fight' mindset driving, we are in defence mode and spend so much time gathering up all the information, evidence, statistics, observations, witnesses and more, to feel like we have enough to protect ourselves in the conversation and prove that we are right prior to going into our imagined 'fight'! We are buried, so stuck in our own head looping around in Own It and Face It that we forget that it's not about us and we lose the entire humanistic side of the conversation as we head into battle.

Our opponent—sorry, I mean team member—or other participant in the conversation senses our emotions, energy and approach and that triggers their defence mechanism, sending them into fight also as they feel they don't have the option to flee. We now have two people in emotional hijacks being driven by their emotional brain (with little to no logic involved) heading into a difficult conversation armed with their defences. How do you think this conversation is going to go?

Chances are there will be very little listening and more just waiting to talk and defend our ground looking for a win in the battle. We don't even think about the outcome we are looking to achieve or that there could possibly be a reasonable explanation. That is all pushed aside as the need to be right and 'win' takes over.

This is the reason I say that overpreparing kills us! We become robotlike on a mission. This is not what a difficult conversation needs. Yes, there should be a bit of preparation, but we are not building a legal case. Instead, look to understand:

- What and when did it happen?
- Who was involved and who was impacted?

- Why did it happen? Why is it an issue?
- How will it be fixed and what is the outcome that we desire?

Keep it simple! Until we hear the other person's answers to these questions, we tend to make some pretty big assumptions. The questions shouldn't be asked like it is an interrogation; they should be genuine questions that we have a non-biased judgement on and are actively listening out for the answer to so we can better understand the situation. Remember, it's a conversation, and a conversation should always start with a simple 'How are you?' Once we know the answers there will be more time to gather the information that is genuinely required to achieve the solution.

While the lead-up and unknown are daunting, actually having the difficult conversation can be nicely broken down into five easy steps:

1. Ask open questions
2. Listen and pause
3. Be empathetic
4. Pose the ultimate question
5. Offer support.

Let's have a look at these in detail.

# 1. Ask open questions

The reason we always start with some form of the question 'How are you?' is to understand what the other person's been through recently and where their current mindset is at.

Remember that your mindset has the power to overturn your logic at any time, so gauging the current state is key. If you hear that the other person is having a terrible day, that their dog is sick and at the vet, now might not be the right time to be discussing their underperformance as you are unlikely to get a supportive response. If their response to you is 'Why do you care how I am?', again you know that the issue is much bigger than underperformance: there is a disconnect and relationship breakdown here that might be underlining the performance issues.

So, simply asking the question 'How are you?' gives you so much information and is the most effective way to approach any difficult conversation because you can respond and guide the conversation based on the emotions at play rather than by following a prepared blueprint.

After 'How are you?', continue with open questions. 'How are you finding work at the moment? How do you think you are going? How do you feel when you wake up knowing it's a workday? What do you like most about your job? How would you describe your current happiness levels in your job? What do you think we can do to improve the performance of the team?' Have a think and list a variety of open questions that you can ask depending on the situation and what is appropriate. Even just reading through these questions will reaffirm that the conversation is not about you; it encourages dialogue and a humanistic approach.

Asking open questions can also break the ice and the intensity (and potential awkwardness) in the room. Never underestimate the value of asking questions and letting the other person speak first. It's like slightly tilting the lid on a saucepan of boiling water and letting some of the steam ease out so that when the lid comes off completely, the steam is not as intense.

## 2. Listen and pause

This really shouldn't require too much explanation. Listening is one of the fundamental basics of any form of communication. This is what makes it a conversation and more than a one-way communication. We don't call them 'difficult messages'—they are 'difficult conversations' and they can't be achieved without letting the other person speak and actively listening. But letting the other person speak and waiting for our turn to speak is not enough. Actively listen to what they are saying *and* the emotion that is driving it.

Following the listening, remember to pause. Pausing and being comfortable with silence is tough for many of us. We have been encouraged to talk since the day we were born so it's natural for us to feel discomfort with silence and feel the need to fill that silence with talking. When we manage to pause, it allows more time for our logical brain to kick in ahead of our emotional brain and to think prior to speaking. It is also very common that the other person will fill that silence by talking, and the longer we pause for, the deeper and more emotionally connected the information they share will be. The easiest way to know when it's your turn to speak is when you are asked a question (or the pause becomes way too long and feels a little creepy!).

This step is interchangeable with step 1. If someone else initiated the difficult conversation, 'Listen and pause' would become step 1, ahead of 'Ask open questions'.

How comfortable are you with pausing and listening? An easy way to build this confidence is to count to three in your head while taking three deep breaths prior to responding or speaking. This allows the other person a chance to talk, it slows down our heart rate and bodily functions and allows more time for the logical brain to kick in ahead of our emotional brain. Give it a go: it will take some practice to build the ability to pause and listen, but the benefits are huge.

# 3. Be empathetic

Empathy: the greatest skill any human being can have! It isn't rocket science but it tends to go against the way our minds are wired. Given we don't naturally love confrontation, when confronted with an intense or unexpected emotion, our mind likes to encourage us to take the easiest way to diffuse the other person's emotion.

Empathy is quite often confused with sympathy, but sympathy is very different. When we feel sympathy, we generally feel sorry for the other person, what they are going through and the situation at hand. There might even be some pity in there. To be empathetic, we don't even have to know what happened that led to the emotional response. Or we could be thinking the other person is completely overreacting and still empathise with them. Empathy is not about putting yourself in someone else's shoes. They are not your shoes — stay out of them!

Even metaphorically speaking, when we put ourselves in someone else's shoes we ask ourselves what we would do or feel and at this point, judgement tends to come with our response: 'Well, I would have done *this* instead to stop it from happening' or 'I don't think it's that bad. Why are they reacting like that?' When it comes to empathy, there is no room for judgement. We don't get to judge the situation or judge whether the emotion on display is appropriate or of the right severity. The only thing we should do is:

- recognise the emotion the person is displaying
- recall when the last time was that we felt that emotion
- ask ourselves 'What is the *worst* thing that someone could have said or done when I felt that emotion?'
- ask ourselves 'What is the *best* thing that someone could have said or done when I felt that emotion?'

Stop reading for a moment and have a think about the last time you were angry. Recall the situation, the feeling, the surroundings, the noises. Take yourself back to that moment...

Now, say out loud the worst thing that someone could have said to you in that moment of anger.

After asking this question to large groups of people for the past five years, I've found that the answer tends to be a resounding 'calm down' or some close variation such as 'take a breath', 'it's okay', 'chill' or 'it's not that big of a deal'.

We know that these are some of the worst things to hear when we are feeling like this. Now recall the last time you had an angry person either in front of you or on the other end of a phone. There is a good chance that your brain was telling you to say 'calm down', or a variation of this that you know would trigger or infuriate you if you were the angry person. Empathy isn't complex; it just tests the natural default response that our brain wants to give.

When our daughter, Amelia, was 15 years old and started her first job at Coles, I can remember how excited I was to see her name on a badge. Our baby girl was growing up! She was most excited about the fact that when you work four hours, they give you a 15-minute break, and Coles pays you for that 15-minute break — unlike many of her friends who worked in fast food and who didn't get paid for the 15-minute break. Now, Coles aren't silly, so the longest shift she had for a few months was a three-hour shift; then she had her first three-hour-and-45-minute shift. Anyway, after her first three-hour-and-45-minute shift, I picked her up from the store, she got in the car and I asked her, 'Babe, how was your shift?' Amelia looked at me and responded with 'Exhausting!' She then went on to tell me that I had no idea how exhausting it is to stand on a checkout (register) for three hours and 45 minutes and smile and talk to people.

At the time, I had just come off a two-day, back-to-back delivery of EI workshops and her reason for exhaustion didn't really sit too well with me. I started to tell her how, actually, my first job while at school was also on a checkout (register), but she stopped me with the good old 'Mum, it's different!' Yes, I took the bait and asked how it was different, and she went on to explain how back in my day (yeah, that hit hard) I didn't have to worry about Flybuys or gift cards or anything like that. Little did she know we didn't even have scanners back then and had to rely on everything having a price tag that we manually put into the register and we had to call for a price check if the tag was missing. I paused and thought to myself, 'Amy, you teach this kind of stuff. What outcome are you looking for here? Maybe try being empathetic.'

So, following the empathy process, I recognised the emotion that she was feeling, which was 'exhausted'. (This was pretty easy as she had specifically told me.) I recalled the last time I was exhausted (I can confirm that it wasn't a three-hour-and-45-minute shift). Then I asked myself, 'What is the worst thing that anyone could say or do to me when I am exhausted?' The answer was to tell me I don't have a right to be exhausted, or that they are more exhausted, or to make it about them — and that's exactly what I was starting to do to her.

I then asked myself, 'What is the best thing that someone could say or do when I feel exhausted?' and that is to listen to me whinge; then go away, give me silent space and leave me alone.

So, I said to Amelia, 'Babe, you seem exhausted.' Even saying the emotion back to her that she had already told me resulted in a massive sigh of relief and a big *yes*, like I really understood and got her.

From there, I asked 'How do we fix this?' Amelia replied with, 'Mum, I just want to go home, soak my shift away in a bath then lie on my bed and watch Netflix.' So that's exactly what we did.

I had a choice in that moment of giving our daughter a reality check conversation of what exhaustion truly was and what working a full day will be like in her future. Just imagine for a moment how our 15-year-old would have responded to that reality check conversation … it's not like she would have turned to me and said, 'Oh Mum, you're right! I'm not exhausted. Silly me, I feel fine. Thanks for the reality check!' Of course that wasn't going to happen. I would be extremely lucky if she even listened to me, let alone took any of it on board.

After an hour and a half of her soaking and watching Netflix, I went to her room and asked her how she felt now. 'Much better, thanks Mum.' I responded with, 'Great, let's have a chat.' At this point, we spoke about the reality of working and that three hours and 45 minutes was not going to be the longest shift she would work and how I might support her to build resilience and give her the tools to adjust. She listened and took it in now that she was no longer in an emotional hijack. Empathy had helped her to break out of it.

Take this into the workplace and picture sitting in a difficult conversation with someone who is feeling angry. Does 'calm down' enter your mind? How would you respond? If someone was upset and started crying, that could be really embarrassing. What would be the best thing for someone else to do for you if you were crying and embarrassed or upset in a work situation? We will talk more about these examples in chapter 11, 'The emotion over the situation'.

Being empathetic every minute of every day is exhausting! I would never say for you to do this in every situation. However, if there are intense emotions in play, empathy will always help you to get the best result for everyone involved. It takes putting your pride aside because it's not about you. It takes no judgement of the situation but rather purely responding to the emotion knowing what it's like to feel that emotion. This is empathy. In situations like difficult conversations, this is the game changer that is often needed.

**The outcome of the conversation should be your focus — not the situation or winning the 'fight'.**

# 4. Pose the ultimate question

This is the absolute magical question for any conversation but especially for difficult conversations: 'How do we fix this?'

The most important word in that sentence is 'we'. It shows we are in this together. There is no us and them; we are united and we are there with them to fix this.

It also helps us to focus on progress and move forward to a solution. The first time we ask the question, they might not hear it and keep talking about the problem or looping in their emotional state, so we ask the question again: 'How do we fix this?' Continue to ask this question until they are ready to move into solution mode. Asking them the question also gives them ownership of the solution and how to achieve it. It can also force them to face and own the fact that it can't be fixed and therefore there is no option other than to accept it, learn from it and move on.

If they provide a solution that isn't realistic, it's important to be honest. Let them know that it isn't an option and try to provide them with a few possible options.

After delivering an EI keynote for a large group of school principals I was asked a question about how to deal with a parent when they are being demanding, rude or unrealistic while you are empathising with them. My response was to ask them the question 'How do we fix this?' and continue to ask it until the conversation moves from the parent either venting or looping in their own emotional hijack to solution mode. In this case the parent was frustrated, angry and wanting time to be reversed to change the outcome, which obviously couldn't happen. Asking them 'How do we fix this?' forces them to own that it has happened and there is nothing that can be done to change it. The next step is to apologise, progress and ensure it doesn't happen again.

When we are feeling an extreme emotion, the majority of the time we know what we want to happen. Rather than trying to guess, ask the question. It can also help to short circuit the emotional hijack.

# 5. Offer support

All difficult conversations should end with 'next steps', including an offer of support: 'How can I further support you?' This creates ownership of and commitment for what we have agreed upon and the actions required.

Expectations should be very clear for everyone involved. Anything that is mentioned or committed to at this stage of the conversation should be documented and everyone involved should be held accountable. Accountability is one of the biggest parts of EI and helps us to avoid ending up in another difficult conversation.

I recently ran a session for a group of leaders who were struggling with difficult conversations. Speaking to several of them one-on-one after the session, it became apparent that their approach to the difficult conversations wasn't too bad. They were following each of the steps but the accountability in step 5 was missing. They weren't holding the other person (or themselves) accountable for the agreed-to and required actions. The actions were set, the support was offered but that's where it ended. They then had to start the process all over again when the same problems re-occurred. Ensure the process is continued well past the end of the conversation and that accountability and follow-up occur.

# Chapter reflection

- Preparation should be kept simple! This is not a battle so keep an open mind, have the right mindset and keep humanity in the conversations.

- There are five easy steps to difficult conversations: ask open questions, listen and pause, be empathetic, pose the ultimate question and offer support.

- These steps should not be scripted but should be a natural ongoing conversation that provides the opportunity to learn information and together reach the best actionable outcome.

- On reflection of the five easy steps, how successful have your past difficult conversations been? What steps are you doing well and what ones will you put more focus on to improve your skills?

# Chapter 11

# THE EMOTION OVER THE SITUATION

While there are hundreds of different emotions and sub-emotions, there are six common emotional responses from people involved in a difficult conversation:

1. upset
2. anger
3. denial
4. meh
5. curiosity
6. positivity.

Each of these emotional responses should be approached in a slightly different way.

The language and emotional undertone of the words that we use can exacerbate the emotion the person is feeling or help own it, process it and move forward. Let's break down each of the emotional responses listed above and discuss what an EI response is, as opposed to things we should be avoiding when that emotion is evident in a difficult conversation.

# Upset

Getting upset or crying during a conversation is not a bad thing. Being upset is no different from any other emotion in that it has an appropriateness and severity levels. We have higher severity levels when fear is driving our emotions or it's something that means a lot to us. Sometimes our hormones can also be out of whack, meaning that we cry more easily than other people (I'm certainly not an expert in this area — just a peri-menopausal woman riding the emotional rollercoaster). Regardless, making fun of someone or complaining about them being a 'crier' or 'getting upset' totally lacks EI.

Here's what I recommend when facing someone who is upset.

- *Best approach:* Getting upset in front of others (especially at work) tends to be embarrassing, so we should respond to the emotion rather than the message we delivered.

- *Ask:* Would you like to take a break, go to the bathroom or get a support person? How can I best support you through this?

- *Things to avoid:* This is not about you — we do not know how they feel because this isn't happening to you. Stay out of your own head and needs. Avoid saying, 'I know how you must be feeling', 'I know this can't be easy', 'I am not loving delivering this message either' — in other words, avoid any sentence that starts with 'I' or is self-related. You don't know how they are feeling, nor should you assume you do. It's not about you at all. When we make statements that start with the letter 'I', it's an obvious sign that we are in our own head, and it's about us rather than them. We don't need to compare or be involved; just listen and provide support based on the emotion of embarrassment or being upset.

# Anger

Anger is an intense emotion that generally puts the person who is angry into an emotional hijack, and quite often the person on the receiving end becomes angry as well. Our mind is being driven by our emotional brain so there is no logic in play and quite often we can't (or won't) hear anything people are saying until the severity decreases or we have finished saying what we have to say.

When facing an angry person, here's what I recommend.

- *Best approach:* Listen and pause! Don't talk. Let them get it off their chest. Once they have aired their frustrations, default to the 'upset' approach, asking them if they would like to take a break or how you can best support them through this. If their anger becomes too much or inappropriate, pause the conversation and let everyone take a break and get back control of their emotions. We should never have to deal with inappropriate levels of anger.

- *Things to avoid:* Our 'fight or flight' response is quite often triggered at this point, so our natural defence mechanism is engaged and ready for battle or ultimate protection. Don't defend or try to justify your reasoning or message. This will only make their defence and anger response even more intense. Remember, you don't need to defend or justify your message. Be confident in what you are saying and doing — quite often less is best here. Given this person is emotionally hijacking, empathy is the best way to help them. Avoid responding with anger too, raising your voice or emotionally hijacking yourself. If at any time, you find yourself doing what you should be avoiding, pause the conversation and let everyone take a break, allowing time for their logical brain to kick in.

# Denial

When our mind doesn't like what we are hearing, we can sometimes go into total denial to avoid the emotion being faced and felt. We put up barriers in our mind to block emotions and truly convince ourselves that this isn't happening so that we feel more protected.

When people are in denial, this is what I recommend doing.

- *Best approach:* Reiterate the facts and reality of the situation clearly and explain the next steps.

- *Ask:* Does what I told you make sense? Do you understand what this means and will result in?

- *Things to avoid:* Some people take time to process and accept information. Trying to force them to do it instantly is never wise and is likely to lead to more denial than them dropping their defence guard. Avoid:

○ getting frustrated with them

○ telling them how to accept it

○ making statements. Ask questions instead to help them process it in their head.

Once you have clearly said everything you need to say and they have confirmed they have heard and understood, reiterate the actions and accountability that will be required.

# Meh

When the care factor or emotional response is low, it can be very confusing. People tend to be 'meh': that feeling of 'couldn't care less' or not being very phased about what is happening. They might seem disinterested or even like they aren't listening.

This is what I suggest you do if you're dealing with a 'meh' reaction.

- *Ask:* Do you have all the information you need? Do you understand the outcome, next steps and expectations? How can I best support you from here? After this, it is best to end the meeting but keep an eye on them and revisit the conversation if required.

- *Things to avoid:* Don't try to make it a big deal if they seem unphased. This might be a cover for a deeper emotion or they might not have processed it yet because it was totally unexpected. Or it may simply not be a big deal to them. Don't keep them there and continue to talk until you get the reaction you want or expected.

The next steps should be very clear and followed through with consequences if required.

# Curiosity

Tough conversations can spark so many unanswered questions, making us curious. Questions aren't a bad thing and are a part of effective communication. Actively listen to their curiosity and answer questions.

Here are my suggestions for managing the questions that curiosity may raise.

- *Ask:* Are there any other questions or thoughts you would like to share? How are you feeling about the information? Do you want to talk about it?

- *Things to avoid:* Don't downplay, avoid or shut down their curiosity. This should not be a one-way conversation. Don't end the conversation before they have finished or have enough answers and information. Avoid making fun of or laughing at any questions or comments.

# Positivity

Sometimes something we believe will be a tough conversation isn't one. For some people, it's a relief to have the conversation or to have the issue out in the open. For others it is an actual 'win' aligned to their priorities (e.g. a redundancy might be what they were hoping for).

While positivity is a good thing, consider the following suggestions for navigating this kind of response.

- *Ask:* Are you happy to share more about what you are feeling and why you are feeling this way? Is there anything more I can do to support you? Keep an eye on them and revisit the conversation if required (especially if the emotion changes).

- *Things to avoid:* A positive response can catch you off guard, so it's important to manage your own emotions both visually and verbally. Avoid:

  ○ cutting the conversation short. Still provide all the details required

  ○ assuming this positive response will stay positive. It may be a protective response and other emotions may follow.

Following the emotion through the conversation brings the humanistic factor back into communication and while it can seem a drawn-out process or distraction, it will get us better interaction, listening, understanding and a better outcome.

# Chapter reflection

- Emotions guide our conversations and can overpower the logical brain. This is why we should approach difficult conversations based on the emotion that is on display rather than the situation.

- If people in difficult conversations are feeling extreme emotions such as embarrassment, blame or feeling attacked, their defence mechanism will kick in and we are unlikely to get the situation resolved successfully.

- Responding to the emotion helps the other person to process and to clear the emotion so that the logical brain can be reengaged.

- On reflection of your emotions over the situation, how do you respond to emotions that occur during difficult conversations? How could you approach them in a better way to get a more desirable outcome to the conversation?

# Chapter 12

# PUTTING IT INTO PRACTICE

If only putting everything into practice was as easy as giving you a template that would work successfully for every difficult conversation, but we all know that every situation and conversation is going to be completely different. What works in one instance won't work in another. The only thing that is going to be similar is the range of emotions felt — that's why we focus so heavily on them. I know it is annoying to hear the good old 'practice makes perfect'. I'm not quite going to endorse that; instead, I will say 'stand up, own your shit and have the conversation!' There is nothing smart about avoiding it, and the excuses (yes, that's what they are) totally lack EI.

While I can't give you a blueprint, I can provide some food for thought around some of the most common difficult conversations for leaders in the workplace. These are:

- underperformance
- redundancy

- unsuccessful job applications
- conflict
- personal issues.

# Underperformance

Underperformance refers to an employee who is not performing at the required and expected level based on their role and compensation. This can be technical (in the field of their expertise), operational (day-to-day performance of tasks) or behavioural (their behaviour towards work, standards/values or other people). Often, we only relate underperformance to technical and operational, but behavioural underperformance is common and should always be addressed. We expect people to perform at a certain level in all aspects and when this level isn't met, they are underperforming.

Underperformance can present in various ways. Dig deeper and ask, 'What is the core concern here?' Whether it is how the person has performed or reacted in a specific situation or whether it is ongoing, either way, it's an underperformance conversation. Sometimes the person is absolutely oblivious to it, but it is still an underperformance conversation.

When this occurs, everyone is impacted! The customers, the team, stakeholders, leaders, management, profitability and so on. Sadly, it is also extremely contagious in that other people will notice and how we choose to respond as leaders will determine the repercussions and how contagious this becomes among the rest of the team. If we choose to look away or ignore it, it will impact the culture and performance of others, and we are sending a message that we are endorsing the underperformance as acceptable. Other team members will start to question why they are performing when there clearly isn't a need to. Our quality and standards will begin reflecting both internally and externally. The first sign of underperformance should always be addressed. It will continue to grow if not addressed and conversations will become a lot more difficult with time, impacting through the layers of business and eventually the culture and company performance.

The first thing we are looking to understand in the conversation is the cause of the underperformance. Is the underperformance the result of:

- lack of skills and/or ability to do the role?
- lack of training?
- lack of care factor or drive?
- poor attitude or behaviour (whether they are oblivious to it or not)?

Each one of these causes will require a slightly different response and actions. Have a think about the possible actions for each response prior to having the conversation. When you get to the 'How do we fix this?' question, the first two causes above (lack of skills or training) are going to have actions for us as leaders to put in place to ensure these needs are met. The other two causes (lack of care factor, poor attitude/behaviour) need to be owned by the team member. They need to answer the questions for us and for their own sake: how will the issue be fixed, can it be fixed and do they want to fix it?

## Remember, don't overprepare!

The purpose of this conversation is not to speak at the team member, pointing out every possible example of underperformance. There is a very good chance that the team member already knows they are underperforming. Sure, you should definitely highlight this and provide examples as part of the conversation, but this is not the purpose of the conversation. The purpose is to understand why it's happened and what the next steps are. You need to understand what outcome you are looking for.

## Ask

Do you want them to turn this behaviour around and start performing? Are you going to provide them with further training? Do you want this person to accept this is not the job for them and leave? Are you putting them on performance management or even terminating them?

The answers to these questions will not be known until the conversation has been had, so be aware that the purpose is to understand the 'why' and the cause of the underperformance and then work through the possible actions or next steps with them. This is going to take great humanistic communication skills, including active listening. This is why overpreparing and going in with a script doesn't tend to work. The mind needs to know the right questions to ask, listen and respond to the emotion, and have possible outcomes ready to discuss based on the learnings that come from the conversation.

The hope is that conversations like this — when we approach them while leveraging our EI — will trigger the other person's EI.

Some open questions to ask are:

- How are things going with work?
- How do you currently feel about your job?
- What are the things you like the best about your job?
- What are the things that really don't interest you about your job?
- How do you think you are currently performing?

These questions are aimed at getting them thinking — to hopefully engage their EI and ownership. If we can get them to own and voice that they are underperforming, this is a massive step in the conversation because we then become their guide/coach. We can then help them by going through the empathy stage — How do we fix this? — and support steps.

But this doesn't always happen. If the team member is absolutely oblivious to their underperformance or in total denial and becoming defensive, we implement the 'Ask, Ask, Tell' method to push them to Own It. This involves asking great questions (like the ones above) twice to encourage their EI to kick in. We do this twice because we are all human and sometimes once is not enough for us to really understand it. But we should only ask twice because if there is still absolute lack of ownership and we continue to ask, we will slowly lose respect and leadership authority, whether intentionally or unintentionally, through the subconscious mind. They could even get frustrated that we are asking again and not listening to them.

After asking twice with no show of ownership, we flick to 'Tell' mode. At this point, we discuss the standard and expectations of anyone in that role and highlight the gaps where the team member is not meeting the standards and expectations.

An example approach is:

- 'The role of sales manager comes with the following expectations ... ' (state the expectations)
- 'Currently, the performance we are receiving from you is not at this level and is instead at this level ...' (state current performance level)
- 'How do we fix this?'

I would make a second attempt at this stage to get them to engage their EI and own the reality and actions. If they still dispute it, deny it or make no effort to take ownership, 'Tell' again: 'This is what I expect from you by ... ' (set a date and list the actions clearly).

Highlighting the expectations is not enough. An action plan should be set then and there, along with clear outcomes, and the consequences, should the outcomes not be fulfilled, made clear. Remember, our mind will always weigh up 'What do I stand to gain?' vs 'What do I stand to lose?' and this will influence whether we commit and truly follow through with ownership.

This is not the end of this conversation. The next meeting should be confirmed along with a regular check-in meeting to review progress against the action plan and consequences.

# Redundancy

In all my years of leadership, making a person redundant was one of the hardest emotional things I had to do. In my situation, the person was a great performer, a great person, was happy with his job, had debt and no intention of leaving. It was simply a change in business and product focus that meant his role was no longer required. This was so tough to deliver! As leaders, sometimes there are tough business decisions that we don't entirely believe in or have any say in. This won't always be a redundancy; it could be any business decision that we are not completely on board with but still need to communicate. It's important to ask our leaders as many questions as possible to get to the point where we own the reality of the situation. If there are any doubts or cracks whatsoever in this ownership, other people will see straight through us and question it as well.

I can remember having a lengthy discussion with my senior executive around the decision and we brainstormed together whether there was any way to avoid the redundancy or even to offer the team member a new role within the business. Unfortunately, after a while we both had to accept that there wasn't. There was nothing else we could do or had control over, and it was time to own the reality that this was going to happen, and it required me to 100 per cent own the communication delivery. I had to face all my emotions and get them right in my head.

Now this does not mean turning our emotions off! To not have any emotion or humanistic qualities when delivering a message like this is a terrible way to be. We can face and process emotions without totally removing emotion. This means we have acknowledged the emotions, know where they are coming from and what belief or value they are attached to, understand why we are feeling this way but also not unpack our bags and stay there. Know that it is what it is, and we must move forward, engaging our logical brain to work together with our emotional brain.

As I moved through the Own It and Face It of the EI process, it was time for me to get out of my own head and Feel It. There was still a possibility that this person could respond with any of the six common emotional responses so preparing and trying to work out how they were going to respond wasn't the be all and end all. My listening and awareness of the emotions during the conversation is where my focus would be required.

## In situations like this, it is best to lead with facts rather than emotion.

While still being a human being and showing emotion, I led with the facts of the business decision: what was happening, why this decision was made, who was impacted, when it would occur and how it would occur. Then I paused to allow time for them to process and Feel It. They now had to get to the point of owning the reality of the situation and face all their emotions. This meant giving them the needed space and time. This person was upset (actually devastated) but understood the reality of the situation. I continued to pause and let them speak and talk through the emotions. Together we then spoke about everything they had achieved and brought to the role and business. We talked about good times and laughed about funny times. There was no need for the question 'How do we fix this?' because it couldn't be fixed. I focused more on 'How can I support you through this process?' I offered to be not only a referee but also to introduce him to connections across the industry where I felt he could add a lot of value. We set up a meeting for the following week to help him develop a plan to find a new job and I did everything I could to help that plan be achieved. At the end of the difficult conversation, he shed a tear, and I followed by shedding a few myself. Was this the right thing to do as a leader? Who knows. Is there a right and wrong way when it comes to this? I was happy to be led by my human side and in that moment, we had a mutual deep appreciation and respect for each other.

Not every redundancy will go like this one went. Some people might welcome a redundancy, making the conversation a lot easier. Others might fight it and respond with anger or even denial. Again, we can't script this. Be aware and read the emotions that are in play. Follow the emotions and respond based on them. Do what it takes to help the person get to the Own It stage then move their way through the rest of the EI process.

## Unsuccessful job applications

Look, I'm not great at deciding on the 'winners' of any situation. In fact, I have actually done a 'Miss America' and announced the wrong winner during a friendly competition in one of my workshops a few years back. I had worked the group up into perfect suspense and asked for a drum roll, only to announce the wrong table number as winners.

I was as shocked as they were when the wrong table started cheering — and everyone in the room was a little shocked as well because there were two stand-out tables and the one I announced was definitely not one of them! It was absolutely horrible, but I owned it then and there and apologised profusely that I had announced the wrong table number. Thankfully they were great sports and admitted that they were shocked too, and we then congratulated the correct winners. They did manage to give me a lot of cheek and remind me at every opportunity of the error I had made and, well, I relived the moment every time. Luckily, we all laughed about it. It's another example of not always getting it right but realising that how we respond makes the difference.

I hope this never happens to you when announcing the outcome of a job application! Deciding on the right candidate or the winner in any situation is tough. Quite often there isn't a perfect candidate. Various people will have great attributes and it's a matter of weighing up the pros with the cons to decide on the best possible fit for right now. Delivering this message is hard, especially if internal people have applied and are involved. This means existing relationships are also at stake.

I had a situation where I interviewed several internal people for a promotion into a new leader role. It came down to two amazing candidates. Both were high performers, I had a great relationship with both and both would bring something very different to the role. They were like each other's yin and yang and that is why they had worked well together for so long. It was an opportunity for each of them to experience their first leadership role. I knew they would both be brilliant leaders and as I write this, both have gone on in their careers to be stand-out leaders in their field! But I had to pick one, regardless of how tough it was, by weighing up exactly what the team needed in a leader right now. What strengths and leadership style were required to be successful? Now that I had this clear in my head it was time for the difficult conversation with the unsuccessful candidate.

Emotions were high. He was shocked and upset, which I totally understood. He also wasn't ready to talk about it right then and needed time to process it. Regardless of what I wanted or had planned for this conversation, the right thing to do was to follow his lead. I didn't end the meeting straight away though. I paused and let him process to see if there was anything else he wanted to say, and I continued to sit there pausing, asking the odd question along the way while he sporadically spat out his feelings and emotions as his emotional brain took over. Empathy was a huge player in this conversation. There was absolutely no need for me to justify or defend my decision. I instead explained the reasoning behind my decision and the thought process, but remained confident in my decision. It wasn't going to change.

Recognising the emotional hijack that he was in was important as it explained his response. Empathy was the number one way to help him move out of the emotional hijack.

Things were rocky for a couple of days — maybe even a week or two. We caught up several more times, giving him the opportunity to ask further questions as he went through the emotional rollercoaster of rejection. We sat down together and updated his development plan for the next 12 months to bridge some of the leadership gaps we'd identified so that he was a step closer to the leadership role next time it was available.

I keep in touch with this amazing human being today, many many years after this situation took place. He is an incredible leader and has grown so much. We reflect on this conversation and on many other difficult conversations we had over the years working together. It makes my heart absolutely sing to hear that he sees just how hard some of these difficult conversations are for leaders and how much awareness and learning he has reflecting on them. He now takes some of the techniques and EI approaches into his difficult conversations as a leader and never avoids a difficult conversation!

# Conflict

Conflict between employees is common and absolutely expected! We can't bring together random people with different backgrounds, interests and brain wirings for (in most cases) five days a week and expect them to all get along. That would be very naïve of us.

Now we all know there are always three sides to every story (the two people involved and the truth) due to unconscious bias.

Sometimes there is a personality clash or disrespect. Work colleagues are not always going to like each other — nor do they have to. They do, however, always need to respect each other and their positions. There will be some relationships that work and some that aren't great. Add to this the fact that some days are shit. It's as simple as that.

Some days, our tolerance is at its final point, and it can be something small that tips us over the edge. This often occurs when we're interacting with someone we don't have a great relationship with — suddenly we've lost our cool, and control of our emotions, over something quite minor. Truth is, sometimes we have nothing in common, and we couldn't be more different in our personalities, interests and approaches. We have a shit day, the other person reacts to this and here we are.

Does this make it right? No, but it explains that it was an unfortunate situation where the emotional brain was likely driving for both of the people involved. Both of them needed to take ownership in this, the role they played in the situation and the consequences. This is going to happen at times — it's reality. It's how we choose to respond that makes all the difference.

There are going to be people who don't have a lot in common and are very different, which can lead to poor relationships and at times conflict. As a leader, sometimes we can see that neither of the people involved are wrong or right. There is simply a personality clash and when this happens, we go looking for things to justify how we feel. It can be the smallest things seen a certain way through one person's eyes that look totally different through the other person's, such as:

- They looked at me with a snarl.

- I saw them whispering to someone and I know it was about me.

- They purposely gave me that piece of work because they didn't want to do it.

- I'm doing way more work than them and they are taking the piss and not doing their job.

- They speak to me with attitude, speak over me, don't listen.

- They are egotistical.

- They gave me a bad review or feedback because they don't like me.

- They didn't invite me to lunch, yet they invited everyone else.

- They override my decisions.

Now, maybe they are right, and it did happen. Maybe they are wrong, and it's been misinterpreted. Either way, it becomes a tough conversation for the leader to address. Too often we avoid these minor conflicts, and they brew and brew and become something far bigger, impacting performance and culture. Resolve these conflicts as early as possible, setting expectations and work on each person to build their EI.

I dealt with many of these kinds of conflicts during my leadership years. Ultimately, it was about sitting them both down, separately at first, to let them vent each of their versions and get things off their chest. I would ask the open questions, listen and pause as they offloaded what was required until their emotional brain could step aside and allow logic in.

### The 'how do we fix this' becomes the number one tool in this situation.

Because, how do you fix a personality conflict? It's extremely hard, so continually coming back to the 'how do we fix this' forces the focus to be on the individuals, the role they played and what they can and can't control.

If the conflict was over performance, each other's performance is not of concern to them and is my concern as a leader, not anyone else's. Now of course, if there was something that should be addressed, as a leader we would default to a separate difficult conversation, but that should play no role in this conflict or conversation. Other team members should not know the details of underperformance or anything that a leader is managing with an individual.

Let each of them know that the other person has no intentions of going anywhere and that you assume they also have no intention of leaving. As such, the reality is that you both work here and therefore must find a way to make this work. So, how do we fix this? It's going to take a few times asking this question because what we are looking for is ownership from both that they are different people, have different wirings and bring different things to the team. It is reminding them that 'other people are not a failed version of us; they are just different and that's okay'. It's a tough pill to swallow when people do things differently from us because it questions whether our way is right and triggers fears that we could be wrong.

Depending on the people involved, there have been times where I have encouraged the two of them to go and grab a coffee together. To have a chat regarding their working relationship and how they can both compromise to make it work. I would never encourage this if there were too much hierarchy or emotion involved as it could make it worse, so read the situation and people well before suggesting this. For the others, the leader should be involved in a three-way conversation to play a mediation role throughout the interaction. The outcome we are avoiding is us telling them what they both must do and how to change. Telling people that they need to change who they are based on a conflict will trigger a defence mechanism and likely make the conflict even worse. It is a compromise — they both need to own the roles each one of them plays in the situation. They don't need to be best friends, but they do need to work together and be respectful to each other and the roles they play. That is the clear expectation from us as leaders and all of us as decent human beings. So, what are they going to do and what will it take? Be nice and make it work.

We offer our support, and some type of follow-up or check-in is definitely needed to see if things are going to plan. Encourage a commitment of honesty and transparency between them both with a civil approach not driven by emotions and in an appropriate environment. This will take commitment and time; but without trust and respect, a relationship won't work, and high performance will never be reached.

## Personal issues

Personal issues are tough! The list that falls into this category can be endless. I've coached people through:

- hygiene issues (odour being a big one)
- inappropriate clothing at work
- behavioural issues
- cultural sensitivity and inclusion
- mental health concerns.

There are so many more and they will continue to arise as every person brings something slightly different to the picture. Regardless, personal issues should be approached in a similar way.

Be completely honest but don't mistake honesty with being nasty or rude. There is no EI whatsoever involved when people make a nasty or rude comment like 'you stink' and respond with 'I'm just being honest' when they are pulled up on it. We can be honest without being straight-out nasty.

We often hope people don't take things at work personally, but these types of issues and difficult conversations are 100 per cent personal so please don't say 'Don't take it personally' because it is!

I wish I had some magical approach to share with you here but there really isn't one. Empathy is going to play a huge role in this conversation. Be very aware of the emotional responses as they change, and let the conversation follow the emotion and empathy rather than the situation. Embarrassment can trigger many different emotions. A lot of these situations are open to interpretation: someone with strong body odour could be as offensive to one person as someone wearing a strong perfume is to another. Given it is so open to interpretation and can quite often be a grey area, it is best to approach the conversation with the facts of what has triggered it and then ask for the team member's thoughts and insights.

For example:

- 'We've received a complaint regarding strong body odour/perfume having an impact on XXX. What are your thoughts on this?' (If there is no impact, question why it is a problem and why they are addressing it.)

- 'I'm unsure if someone has shared our work dress code guidelines with you already. Have you seen them before?' (If there are no guidelines, that's the first problem to address. If the answer is yes, reiterate the guidelines, expectations, impact and consequences).

- 'We have some concerns around your behaviour in some situations. Here are some examples of where it concerned me, the impacts and what I would expect to see instead. What are your thoughts on this?' (If you don't have examples, the conversation shouldn't be happening.)

- 'Cultural sensitivity and inclusion are a prime focus for us. There have been some instances where, I'm not sure if you are aware, your behaviour has had a negative impact in this area. Here are some examples and their impacts. What are your thoughts on this?' (Ensure expectations and consequences are clear before the conversation ends.)

- 'Are you okay? I am concerned about your wellbeing and want to make sure you are okay. How are you feeling? What is one thing that could happen to improve the impact on your wellbeing and mental health? Talk to me about the support network you have in place.'

Please note that any mental health or wellbeing concerns should involve someone appropriately qualified in that area. All leaders should be encouraging the right medical support and not taking it upon themselves to counsel or make recommendations if they are not qualified to do so. The health of the individual should always be put first and sometimes work is exasperating, causing the symptoms, so find out whether they should be at work and whether this is the best job for their health. Again, refer them to their doctor and, if unsure, ask for a doctor's recommendations or clearance.

● ● ●

Given the complexity of the human brain, emotions and people, I can't address every difficult conversation in this book. The five difficult conversations I have provided insight on will give a foundation for you to work from for any difficult conversation.

These are purely examples of things to say to help spark ideas — please don't use them as a script. There is nothing human-like about communicating a difficult conversation based on a script. Understand the person you are speaking to, how they are wired and how they react. Put the emotion over the situation and refer to the tips in the previous chapters on what to say and what to avoid when certain emotions are at play (especially change). Remember, the EI process is always in play.

# Chapter reflection

- There is no blueprint or easy script for difficult conversations. The key is to ask the right questions and not trigger a defensive reaction.

- No-one is perfect and as a leader, we won't always have the answer.

- Sometimes it is about accepting what we can control and compromising to make it work.

- Always be honest and remember what outcome you are looking to achieve.

- On reflection of putting it into practice, what role are you playing in conversations and how successfully are you doing it? How can you build your EI skills to improve conversations? Are there conversations that you can now go and have with a clear mind and a humanistic approach?

# Chapter 13

# MANAGING UP

You've probably heard the terms 'managing up' and 'managing down'. They describe how well we manage relationships and communication with our managers and those in positions higher than us (managing up) and how well we manage them with our direct reports (managing down). The five common difficult conversations we put into practice in chapter 12 relate to managing down. There are many leaders out there who do well with difficult conversations when managing down but it is the difficult conversations when managing up that they get stuck on.

Let's look at managing up and managing down through two different lenses. As leaders, we wear many hats (to use a metaphor) in our different roles and environments. We wear one hat when we are leading our team and another hat as a team member working with managers, stakeholders and peers. Each hat has a different role and requires a different set of skills if we are to be successful in it.

When I am wearing the hat above the line in figure 13.1 (overleaf), I am a team member. It is here that I listen, question, challenge and create strategy. This is the time to work on self-development and growth—the development plan. We build stakeholder, peer, leader and top-level manager relationships. Together, our team is all on the same page, aligned and with a united front. This is what it feels like to wear the leadership team hat above the line skilfully.

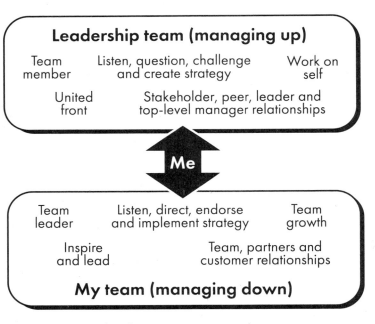

**Figure 13.1:** as leaders, we wear many hats

When I put on my team hat sitting below the line in figure 13.1, my focus and skills change. Now I am a team leader. I listen, provide direction, endorse the messages I am delivering and implement strategies. The growth I am focused on is my team's growth and development plans. Relationships I am building are with my team, partners and customers. I am there to inspire and lead my team to high performance and success.

We tend to measure our leadership success based on the hat below the line, but the hat above the line is equally important. It helps us to be a better leader when wearing the hat below the line.

## Ask

How well do you wear both hats? Take a moment to think about the focus and time you dedicate to both hats. If you were to rate yourself out of 10 for both hats, with 10 being 'you are absolutely brilliant at it', what would your score be in each hat? What is one thing you could do to increase the score in each hat?

## Communication competencies

When we are wearing the top hat, difficult conversations change and before we even worry about the actual conversation, we need to reflect on ourselves, our competencies and our ability to manage up.

Figure 13.2 (overleaf) illustrates how those competencies change depending on the hat we are wearing. Mastering the competencies of managing up will decrease the number of difficult conversations we have to have and will help to provide solutions. The more we build these competencies, the fewer difficult conversations will be required and our managing up relationships will grow, creating more balance and less misalignment.

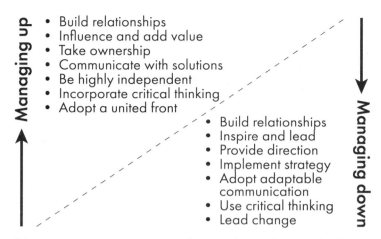

**Figure 13.2:** competencies change depending on the hat we are wearing

## Build relationships

Managing up, our relationships with our manager, our manager's manager and the people above them are just as much our responsibility as the relationships we build when managing down. Too often I hear leaders say that they never hear from their leader or from the CEO or anyone in the C-Suite. My first question back is, 'When was the last time you made the effort to contact them?' Relationships are a two-way street. Yes, everyone should be making an effort but there is only one thing we can control in this world: ourselves. We can't control the effort that others make but it is a big self-reflection piece for us to complain and point the finger if we haven't made any effort either. Take ownership and do something about it. If these relationships are poor, bad or non-existent, expect repercussions in all other areas. Also expect misalignment, lack of trust and difficult conversations. We have got to own the role we play in all our relationships. If we are not happy with how a relationship currently stands, do something about it, regardless of your position and their position. Be a decent human being and create the connection. If the connection isn't great, the expectations and respect for each other should always be clear.

If I asked your CEO whether they know you, what would they say? Would it be 'yes'? Yes, for the right reasons or yes for the wrong reasons? Or would it be 'no, I haven't heard of them'. Your reputation is in your hands — you can influence it, so start today. What have you done to build this relationship? What can you do right now to build this relationship? A difficult conversation is always going to be harder when there is no established relationship or expectation.

## Relationships are the foundation of every interaction.

## *Influence and add value*

As a leader representing a team or department of the organisation, we have insights, information and skills that can add value to conversations and influence decisions. When wearing our top hat, we should never be a seat warmer. We are there for a reason and that reason should be to add value as a team member and influence decisions. I hear leaders complaining or unhappy about something that has happened at that higher level but when I ask them did they flag it, mention it or put a different option on the table based on their beliefs, quite often the answer is no. If the answer is yes but it didn't make any difference, then own the reality and move on.

People sitting in executive or senior leadership positions are pictured as having high intelligence and sometimes even as being the 'high and mighty'. In truth, they are just human beings, the same as us. They don't always have the answers, but they will make decisions based on the information they have. If we don't provide input, or add value to the conversation, they don't know what they don't know. We are sitting at that table to contribute and share knowledge of the possible impacts and outcomes when decisions cascade through our teams. Yes, we hope that the other people sitting around the table will leverage their emotional intelligence and remember to 'Feel It' and 'Ask It' but if they don't, it is our job to bring this up and influence them at any opportunity we can.

## Take ownership

The core of EI is taking ownership. This should be done at every level of who we are. Our mind is so quick to look for other people to blame or other people to take responsibility. Again, we reiterate ownership when managing up. There is always some type of action we can take to improve a situation. It may not change the original decision but it can make the decision a little easier to process or work with. When we are in any form of middle management, the temptation is there to simply be a messenger between the front line and upper management. This shouldn't be the case. As middle managers we should be looking at all situations being fed up to us as a problem requiring ownership and a solution by us. The so-called 'buck stops with us'. It is our opportunity — and really our role — to stop the problem there at our level and manage back down the solution. Should the idea or solution require sign-off or input from upper management, then we always table the problem with ownership together with a proposed solution.

## Communicate with solutions

Communication is an absolute given but remember that communication is a two-way interaction. It's not just about being reactive to the requests for communication that come from above. It's about being proactive with our communication and providing information through reports, updates and any form of communication that provides insights into how our team/department are doing in line with our goals and the company strategy. There should be some type of formal or informal agreement between leaders of what the expectation is when it comes to communication for both parties. This should include the frequency, the communication platform (for example, email, report, phone call, meeting), why it is important, the expectations of how it will look and what it will include.

These communications should be a complete picture — from the problem, idea or situation through to the solution. Each one does not need to be a multi-page business case, but remember our minds are always looking for 'what do we stand to gain vs what do we stand to lose'. If this isn't outlined as a minimum, the conversation is going to be very short and will likely end up with a negative response, if any.

When we are communicating with others, very few people are looking for extra work to take on from the communication, so we want to get the communication to the point where all our manager needs to respond with is a 'yes' and that we have already proposed all of the details around the what, when, how, why and who. Saying 'yes' means they don't have to do any work. A problem or improvement has been arranged and it's one less thing to talk back and forth on. Make it as easy as possible for them to say yes. If it is half done or is going to require them going away and doing something, we are creating a delay, adding to their workload and making it easier for them to say 'no' than to say 'yes'. Always communicate with a solution.

## Be highly independent

As a leader, when we can be absent from our team and the team steps up empowered and takes control, we know we are succeeding and our team is performing well. This is the same with us. When we are wearing the top hat and are a member of a team, our growth and development is about being that team member who can step up empowered and do our job without a heavy reliance on our leader. This is how we know we are succeeding in our role as a high performer. This requires a high level of independence that is built from competency and confidence, both of which are areas that should be highlighted in our development plans and be part of our growth markers.

Team members who require constant assistance from their leader, either asking excessive questions, asking for opinions or copying them into every email and communication, don't project a lot of independence and confidence. As we move into higher levels of leadership, being highly independent is not just an expectation, it's a must-have. You need to be able to perform at a high standard independently as well as a team member.

Are you highly independent or involving your leader in absolutely everything?

## Incorporate critical thinking

Critical thinking is the skill that sits at the core of each of the areas we have just discussed. While there are many different definitions and steps to critical thinking, I like to reference Monash University's definition:

> Critical thinking is a kind of thinking in which you *question, analyse, interpret, evaluate* and *make a judgement* about what you read, hear, say or write.

The Monash critical thinking model takes us through six core skills:

1. Clarify your thinking purpose and context.
2. Question your sources of information.
3. Identify arguments.
4. Analyse sources and arguments.
5. Evaluate the arguments of others.
6. Create or synthesise your own arguments.

We can see simply by looking at these six core skills of the model the level of detail that goes into making quality decisions and really taking ownership into our own hands before communicating and taking action. Without critical thinking, we lose the substance to our decisions and communication.

Building this skill makes managing up easier in every situation.

## Adopt a united front

One of our biggest downfalls is to only see our 'team' when managing down and think that this is the only team we should be focused on. We always have peers who are also middle managers. Yes, they might have completely different expertise or departments from us, but they will still be faced with similar people problems and management situations. Too often when we are managing up, we don't see the other people around the table as our team. Each of us goes in on behalf of our own team and becomes quite pushy or defensive to get the best possible outcome for the team that we manage down. This makes the environment where we are wearing that top hat very competitive, self-absorbing and self-driven. It creates conflict and competition internally rather than a united team that is making decisions based on what is best for the organisation.

I was working with a senior leader team early in 2024 and it was fascinating that when they came together for the program, it was one of the first times they had ever all been in the same room together. They definitely didn't see themselves as one team and were very region focused and divided. Decisions and requests were pushed based on what was good for their team and region. What was happening in the other teams or regions was not really of concern or focus. They were all working individually fighting the same challenges separately and not leveraging the strength of the national team together.

One of the biggest wins out of the six-month program was to see that at the end they were making decisions with a united front. Some of the senior leaders who had been so focused on their own agendas at the beginning of the program were now leaning in and providing resources to other regions. It wasn't that they had extra resources or because their teams were up to date; it was simply because while everyone was struggling, the impact on the brand and market in some regions was far greater based on the competitive market. Their region could afford to be a further day behind in its work knowing the impact would be very little and the acceptance from their market would be there. Having to have that kind of turnaround in another region could have had dire impacts and would risk the business as a whole losing a large portion of its portfolio to a competitor. This is what a united front looks like. It's coming together as one team to support each other. If a team of four people have 40 outstanding pieces of work, that's 10 extra pieces for each person. However, if you leverage the national team, which has more than 40 people, that's less than one extra piece of work per person and your backlog is gone.

## A united approach is a smart approach.

A united front is not just working together; it's communicating together as well. While wearing that top hat, we not only listen but also challenge. This means we won't always get our way or the outcome we were hoping for. A decision will be made, and we will own whatever that decision is — that's the reality. When we turn around to our team and manage down, we must be 100 per cent onboard with the decision. Whether it was what we wanted or what we thought no longer matters — the decision is reality and if our team can see any crack whatsoever in our belief or if we are not 100 per cent okay with it, they too won't be. Quite often there isn't a perfect answer to any situation so there are always going to be pros and cons. The decision made should be the best outcome at the time, weighing up these differences. Don't get caught up on the cons; be transparent about the decision and be onboard. When decisions are made at that managing-up level, everyone involved must be united.

# They are still not listening

If we have approached a difficult managing-up conversation, leveraging and building our core skills in all the above areas and with every tool for difficult conversations and we are still faced with a 'no' or a leader who is not listening or being emotionally intelligent, there is only one thing left to do: apply our EI to ourselves and Own It.

The reality is that the only thing we have control over in life is ourselves and how we choose to react. We can build our skills and competencies and approach the situation with every tool ready to go, but if there is no way to get through, well, there is no way to get through!

It's time for us to Own It. Own the reality of the situation. Own that we gave it absolutely everything we could, and that this is the outcome and reality of the situation. It's not going to change, and we can either accept this, move on and work with what we do have, or we can walk away. It's a tough call but it is sometimes that reality that we ignore or avoid.

Face the emotions that are rolling in our mind and where they are coming from. Weigh up our different options — what we stand to gain vs what we stand to lose — until we process the emotions and are ready to move forward.

Feel and understand the impact on those around us and what opportunities will arise for them to be empowered or how we can support them through it.

Ask the right questions to trigger and balance our logical brain with our emotional brain so that we know the exact steps and logistics needed to make it happen.

Drive It and take action. This is us taking back control knowing again that the only thing we really have control over is ourselves and how we choose to respond. Sometimes knowing that this is no longer a good fit for us isn't a bad thing. It's not anyone's fault — it's just time for all of us to move on. They haven't made us leave or make this decision; we have made it based on our own values and beliefs. It's time to accept and move forward with our decision.

## Chapter reflection

- Managing up and managing down successfully requires different skill sets. As leaders, we should be working on developing ourselves in all these skill sets.

- Communication and relationships are key when managing up. We can't change other people, but the way in which we communicate, interact and perform always impacts the outcome.

- When we still don't feel like we are making progress, we should always default to the EI process, starting with Own It!

- On reflection of managing up, where are your skill gaps and what will you do to bridge these gaps?

# Chapter 14

# REFLECTION

Like all areas of EI, we won't get every difficult conversation right every time. Every single one of us has an emotional brain and inbuilt fears that, even with the best intentions, will get triggered in certain situations and we find ourselves not being so emotionally intelligent. I get it—it's reality and we must Own It.

It's our reflection and response when it doesn't work that determines the outcome. If we are lucky enough to become aware of our wrongdoings while they are happening, it's having the ability to pause, take three deep breaths, get our thoughts back together and apologise for what we did or said that was wrong. 'I'm sorry. I lost control of my emotions there, and it was wrong and inappropriate. Can I try that again?'

If it takes a reflection to become aware of our wrongdoings, it is never too late to apologise. It doesn't matter if it's minutes, months or years later. The other person can remain impacted for years until they hear those simple words: 'I'm sorry. I was wrong' or 'I was out of line'. When someone does something wrong, we want to know that they are aware of it and own it. We generally get that no-one is perfect, but please show us that you are taking ownership of it, apologising and responding to make it better.

During reflections, I like to ask myself five simple questions:

- What went well?
- What didn't go so well?
- What will I do better next time?
- What actions will I take to rectify the situation based on the role I played in what didn't go well?
- What do other people need from me now to achieve a good outcome?

Reflection is our number one opportunity for growth and development yet it is frequently overlooked as we search for brand new learning opportunities. It's like focusing on new customers and not caring about the existing ones. The big picture is not going to be great, and we are running around in a vicious circle wondering why the same outcomes keep happening.

Take the time to reflect either on a daily, weekly, fortnightly or monthly basis. I would always recommend a minimum of weekly. Whether it's reflecting on a difficult conversation or simply asking ourselves the question, 'How emotionally intelligent was I today/this week? What can I do to improve this tomorrow/next week?'

## Chapter reflection

- Reflecting is the ultimate opportunity for growth! This is why I have a reflection question at the end of every chapter. Take the time to stop and reflect!

- We won't always get it right, it's how we choose to respond when we don't get it right that shows our true levels of EI.

- On reflection of this chapter, are you nailing the power of reflection? What will you put in place to grow through reflection?

# Part IV

# HIGH-PERFORMING TEAMS

We hire people to do a job to their best ability. This level of ability will vary depending on the person and the job. When we bring a team of people together, we are looking to create a balance across the ability and level of skills so that the team members bounce off each other and support each other's strengths and weaknesses. As the relationship of the team grows, so too does the performance until they reach peak performance with a great culture.

High-performing teams is what we all strive to achieve. I'm a huge fan of the TV series *Ted Lasso*. The reason why I bring this up is because the character Ted Lasso depicts a leader who leverages EI to be a high-performing leader, create a high-performing team and be a great human being. A high-performing team doesn't always mean that they win every match or that they get it perfect every time. It does mean that they are aligned, with a common purpose and direction. That they have relationships across the team. They know they won't always get it right, but they will Own It and talk about it.

When 'high-performing teams' is mentioned, there are many teams and brands around the world that we think of. Have a think about who you would identify as being a 'high-performing team' within your industry, across your country and throughout the world.

## Ask

What are the attributes that make them high performing? How does your team compare? Would outsiders identify your team as being high performing? How could your team come one step closer to being a high-performing team?

These are great questions to brainstorm with your team. Get them thinking about the current state of the team and what it will take to be a high-performing team in their eyes.

A high-performing leader and team means three key factors resonate with every person in the team:

- team alignment
- trust
- communication.

I have already discussed aspects of communication in detail. In part IV I'll explore the other two key factors that make up high-performing teams: alignment and trust.

# Chapter 15

# TEAM ALIGNMENT

Having alignment within a team means everyone being on the same page, understanding the vision, the purpose of the team, the values, the goals and the behaviours, and knowing how these all connect from a team level to an organisation level. This alignment helps to create unity across the team. While everyone in the team performs a different role and has different tasks and strengths, alignment means they have a common vision, purpose, value, goals and behaviours to come together as one and achieve the desired outcome. If there is misalignment in any of these areas, the team's performance and success will become questionable.

It is the leader's responsibility to communicate and build this alignment within the team, helping each team member to own the role they play in the big picture and be committed to making the desired outcome happen. This should be done by ensuring that every team member has a detailed understanding of the organisation's strategy and what it stands for.

In this chapter, I will break down what it takes to create team alignment by:

- having a clear understanding of the company strategy and the three main areas of balanced leadership
- ascertaining how to be a strategic leader and create vision and direction for your team
- identifying your time spent in operational leadership and whether it is efficient and effective
- creating foundations and expectations within people leadership to ensure a high-performing culture.

## Business strategy

It astounds me how many organisations don't have a business strategy or a 'Strategy on a Page' (SoaP). A SoaP is a simplified overview of the business strategy that fits on one page. It includes the purpose, vision and strategic/key areas of focus and values/behaviours. A business strategy document can be many pages long, also detailing the data behind the SoaP, the initiatives and actions that will deliver the business goals.

The team should be able to see the direction of the business by reading the SoaP and everything else in the business should have alignment to the SoaP.

Any initiative, idea or allocation of budget should be communicated with the business strategy in mind showing how doing 'this' will lead to achieving 'this' in the strategy. Sometimes we will come up with great ideas and initiatives, but if there isn't a clear alignment to the business strategy then maybe now is not the time for it to be done.

The business strategy provides a scope of works that the business will be focused on achieving during a specified span of time. This is the priority for the business and should represent every part of the business.

Without clear direction, expectations and identity, the business risks misalignment and poor relationships between organisation layers, departments, stakeholders and people.

**To be a great leader and create alignment, the leader needs to have balance across their leadership role and tasks.**

# Being a balanced leader

Being a leader is about so much more than getting the job done. Quite often, when someone becomes a leader through promotion, they continue to get 'stuck in the weeds'; that is, the day-to-day work. They remain quite hands on with respect to their previous job tasks and are reactive to situations and people rather than creating a strong foundation for the team as a balanced leader through direction, expectations and identity. This is common where a leader starts in a technical role and is promoted to a leadership role — for example, a highly trained medical professional who then becomes a leader of people. It can be difficult to step back from doing the 'hands-on' technical aspect of what they have been extensively trained for to be a balanced leader.

A balanced leader is one who understands that they need to allocate time to each of the three main aspects of leadership:

- strategic leadership
- operational leadership
- people leadership

I don't mean reactive time; I mean planned, proactive work as a leader. In this chapter, we will look at all three of these leadership aspects and how to create strong foundations in each area.

Based on how you currently lead, ask yourself, 'What would the percentage split be across all three aspects?' There is no right answer here…although if any of the areas are below 10 per cent, there are gaps in your leadership that will be impacting your team and their performance. The percentage split will vary depending on your leadership role, the size of the team, the industry you work in and your job description. However, to be any kind of leader, you should be aiming for a minimum of 10 per cent of your time being spent on each of the three aspects of leadership. Where the rest of the split lies is completely up to you and depends on your goals.

Here's a rundown on each of the three leadership types.

## *Strategic leadership*

Strategic leadership refers to the 'big picture' of the team and alignment with the organisation's current and future direction. Every organisation needs a strategy that documents the business goals, actions and initiatives; and the long-term vision of the organisation. To be an emotionally intelligent leader, you must have a clear understanding of and make a contribution to the company vision as well as ensuring your team are familiar with this vision and are 100 per cent on board. As the leader, you are the voice that contributes both up and down the line to create alignment between your team and the organisation. Bring this to life through team strategy and planning days involving your team. Reference every initiative that the team does back to the strategy and connect the role they play in achieving it. If the company vision or strategy is not clear to you or your team, this is the first area to focus on. Ask questions and dig deep with your managers until you have a clear understanding.

There are several ways to bring strategy into your day-to-day work, enabling your team to step back from operations and connect the dots. This can be done by:

- *resolving complex problems through discussions or 'pain point meetings'.* A pain point meeting is a meeting dedicated to everyone tabling their biggest pain point and the team working together to brainstorm opportunities to resolve these that align directly to the strategy. Using the strategy as a guide to first understand what strategic/key area of focus it belongs under, then bridging the gap of what is required to move towards the initiatives and desired outcomes, will help to resolve the problem

- *identifying threats using a SWOT (Strengths, Weaknesses, Opportunities and Threats) analysis.* The team does this as a collective, really opening their minds and including all ideas. Don't cull or disregard anything; every thought or idea should be voiced and documented in the brainstorm.

- ○ Start by listing all the strengths of the team. What makes this team so good? What is the team doing well? What skills do the team have?

- ○ Then move on to the weaknesses. Where are we not doing so well? What works against us? What are our downfalls?

- ○ Next look for the opportunities that can be identified in the team. What could we focus on that will strengthen the team? What ideas would improve our performance and results?

- ○ Last is the threats. What would impact our ability to do our job well? What are our competitors doing? What external factors, change or challenges are potential risks (e.g. environmental, government)?

The SWOT outcomes provide a balanced capability reflection and idea projection for the team to work with and create its own strategic direction.

See figure 15.1 for a sample SWOT analysis grid.

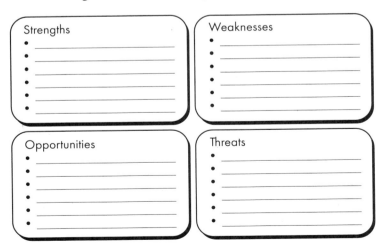

**Figure 15.1:** SWOT analysis grid

**Ask**

How much time are you spending in strategic leadership? Do you have a thorough understanding of the company strategy? Are you sharing this strategy with your team? Can you explain how your team contributes to the strategy?

The percentage of time spent in strategic leadership will increase the higher your leadership role is. By senior and executive level, it could become the greatest portion of your time, but every leader should be spending some time in this space.

## Operational leadership

This is the day-to-day function and performance of the team. It's in this space that we manage workflow, create measurable key performance indicators (KPIs) or targets, and show how they flow from the strategy down to the teams and then to the individuals. Be transparent with progress around these targets, remembering to celebrate the wins, create goals and reflect to resolve the losses.

The execution of the goals will be reliant on the team members having a clear understanding of their roles and strength alignment to these goals. Managing and leading operations is done through daily management and planning, including:

- change intelligence, communicating and implementing change aligned to the change intelligence model detailed in part II

- workflow and resource management, managing the daily tasks across team members supported by some type of reporting platform to create transparency and assist with planning

- creating efficiency through innovation and improvement activities such as a simple 'Keep, Stop, Start' (brainstorm the following three questions with the team: What will we keep doing?, What will we stop doing? and What will we start doing?)

## Ask

How much time are you spending in operational leadership and is it too much? What will you do to improve efficiencies and empower your team to decrease your 'hands-on' time in the daily operations?

Front-line and middle managers tend to spend a large amount of time in operational leadership—rarely ever less than 10 per cent. Quite often, it is the area in which they can get caught up spending way too much time involved in the daily operations of strategic and people leadership. Leaders should be building the team through empowerment in operations, which is a win for the team members and a win for the leader, freeing up their time spent in this part of their role.

## *People leadership*

Ahhh, my favourite area! This is an absolute given part of being a leader but it can be a very tough gig, especially when a lot of it is reactive to what is happening in the moment with people and situations. When we look at the time percentage split, we should be talking about planned proactive time in this space. There will always be people leadership time that is reactive — such as resignations, recruitment, performance issues and conflict — but the reactive time in this space tends to increase when proactive time is not happening. If we get the proactive framework in place, it naturally decreases the reactive people leadership challenges via risk mitigation.

It's in this space that we:

- manage all levels of performance through structured performance reviews and regular conversations, transparent and realistic measures, and targets and progress. These performance measures should be directly aligned to achieving the organisation's strategy and should be communicated clearly and understood. Failure to do this tends to result in underperformance and a difficult conversation. The longer we leave this, the worse the impact and the more difficult the conversation will become. No-one should ever get to an annual performance review and not know where they stand. By the time the annual review is completed, they should have received a clear summary of their performance over that year and agreement on where they have landed following the monthly discussions. Nothing should be a surprise in this meeting!

- identify the talent and succession, and implement strategies to keep those identified as current or future talent. The talent matrix '9-box grid' (see figure 15.2, overleaf) is a fantastic tool that helps to map the potential vs performance of each team member, identifying the overall level of talent. It helps the leader to know how to work with each person and who are potential successors based on their position in the grid. The succession planning should be an ongoing process and built into development plans so that when the need arises, the training is already underway or even completed

- create meaningful development plans with three suggested goals per annum and monthly catch-ups to discuss progress and performance. When I say *meaningful* development plans, I really mean *meaningful* development plans. This should not be a generic, tick-a-box template where you state, 'Yes, there is a development plan once a year' when asked. That means absolutely nothing to the leader or the employee. This also shouldn't be leader-created. It should be owned and managed by the employee, but it is the leader's role to ensure it exists, it is meaningful, and conversations happen every month to track progress and performance

- gauge and monitor the culture status of the team, including work engagement levels and the general vibe on a regular basis. The 'Sunday night test' is an easy question to direct at the team: ask them how they feel on Sunday night knowing they have to go to work the next day. (Psychological safety is another important area and I will talk about this in detail in chapter 16, where I discuss trust.)

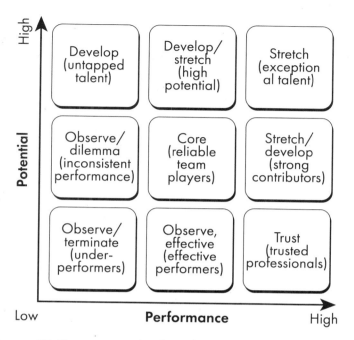

**Figure 15.2:** an example of a 9-box grid

Sadly, this is the part of leadership that tends to be dropped or pulled back when time pressures occur, but it's a catch-22. Decrease the proactive people leadership and expect to see the reactive leadership increase with resignations, conflicts, underperformance, personal issues and pretty much every type of difficult conversation that can occur. It takes far less time to do proactive people leadership and set clear expectations than it does to fix reactive people leadership, have difficult conversations and mend culture. It's our choice which path we take, and we own the outcomes we face based on this choice.

## Ask

How much time are you spending in proactive people leadership? Have you got a clear and documented framework so that any leader could walk into your team and know where your team are at, how they are performing, and what their development and future succession planning looks like? If the answer isn't a confident 'yes', start by dedicating even a few hours each week on a set day to proactive people leadership.

High-performing teams have leaders that are balanced and aligned across all areas of leadership. They don't excel in just one area but in all three of the following:

- the strategic direction and vision of the organisation's goals
- the support, planning and management of daily operations
- the people leadership management and structures to have a culture with strong relationships and clear expectations.

# Chapter reflection

- High-performing teams have clear alignment across their purpose, vision, performance and expectations detailed in the organisation's strategy.

- Being a great leader means balancing your leadership skills and time across all three areas of leadership: strategic, operational and people.

- On reflection of team alignment, how will you improve the percentage of time you currently spend in each area of leadership? What actions will you schedule to create strong foundations in all three areas of leadership?

# Chapter 16

# TRUST

Trust is at the heart of everything we do. The level of trust we have in a person, in a situation or in ourselves influences whether an outcome will be positive and what we might expect. Trust is one of the common traits called out in high-performing teams, yet it can be tough to define. Empowerment relies completely on our ability to trust that the other person is ready to be empowered. Relationships outside of work are also built on trust. We know that this word 'trust' is important, and it drives so much of who we are and what we do, but what does it actually mean?

Charles Feltman's definition of trust is one of my favourites, and his book *Thin Book of Trust* is a great read. Feltman defines trust as:

> choosing to risk making something you value vulnerable to another person's actions. Distrust is deciding that what is important to me is not safe with this person in this situation (or any situation).

I love that this definition gets deep into the vulnerability of sharing something truly valuable and important to us. Remembering that our fight-or-flight mechanism is guided by our sense of safety and security, it's natural for us to be always looking for that sense of safety in people or environments.

Trust and distrust run as two parallel networks within our brain. Trust provides a feeling of safety and openness, and a desire to connect and create together with others. It triggers increased levels of oxytocin (also known as the love hormone) and activates the prefrontal cortex, helping to regulate our amygdala (emotional brain), where the fight-or-flight response lives.

Distrust provides feelings of fear, suspicion and defensiveness. It triggers increased levels of cortisol and testosterone, telling us that there is danger or threat, and activates the fight-or-flight response within us. Other people are seldom as big of a danger or threat as our mind thinks, but distrust is our defence mechanism to feel in control.

In this chapter we will learn that understanding the mind's reaction to trust and distrust is based on the two different forms of trust: environmental trust and individual trust.

# Environmental trust

Environmental trust is when the trust element refers to our surroundings. Do we feel safe? Do we trust that this environment is the right one for us? In the workforce, we weigh this up in terms of our psychological safety and our cultural agreements.

When it comes to influential thinkers in psychological safety, the global leader would have to be Professor of Leadership at Harvard Business School, Amy C Edmondson. The work that Edmondson has done, and continues to do, in this space is continually growing throughout workplaces around the world as we realise how deep the impact of psychological safety is on people's wellbeing and the success of the organisation. Based on Edmondson's work, psychological safety is a shared belief that it's okay to take risks, express ideas and concerns, speak up or admit mistakes without fear of negative consequences.

Edmondson's work, and in particular the seven questions to understanding psychological safety that she developed, is a fantastic basis for looking at how psychologically safe people feel in their workplace environment. Edmondson's seven questions enable individuals to feel psychologically safe by assuring them that:

- if you make a mistake on this team, it is not held against you
- members of this team are able to bring up problems and tough issues
- people on this team sometimes accept others for being different
- it is safe to take a risk on this team
- it isn't difficult to ask other members of this team for help
- no-one on this team would deliberately act in a way that undermines your efforts
- working with members of this team, your unique skills and talents are valued and utilised.

It is important to note that these points should not be taken solely at face value because interpretation and emotion will play a large role for each person. There is no 'right' or 'wrong' when it comes to how someone feels, so the real work happens when we start to understand why they feel that way.

Any measure that we can get on how people are feeling at work provides a benchmark as well as opportunities for areas to focus on to increase those measures and create an increase in the overall psychological safety of the environment. If this is a very new area for you, start by having an open conversation with your team about what psychological safety is and why it's important to you and the organisation. The industry we work in can come with a societal expectation of trust or distrust, which will play into whether this expectation is being met or not. For example, we have a high trust in doctors and people in high-profile professions, whereas our trust for salespeople — especially car salespeople — and insurance companies is much lower. This is not to say these societal norms are right or wrong. They simply exist for us based on our upbringing and experiences and should be taken into account when looking at the level of trust in the internal and external environment.

Encourage conversations and create an anonymous survey and opportunities for people to talk in private about their psychological safety. Understand what your team's psychological safety score looks like by tallying the score and working out the average. Utilise the responses from these conversations and questionnaires to ask, 'How might we improve the psychological safety in this specific area?' and, together with your team, create an action plan. It begins with starting the conversation around psychological safety and having a genuine desire to create a psychologically safe environment.

'Cultural agreement' is a fancy way of describing the behaviours and environment that your team as a collective deem to be acceptable. It might include a code of conduct, an ethical agreement or behaviour norms.

**Culture is the outcome of a group of people interacting together. It isn't tangible, so it can't be fixed as such.**

The only way to improve it is for each person involved to work on themselves. To improve ourselves or our culture, we need to first agree on what is the accepted norm for our culture. What are the expectations that we have on ourselves and the people around us when it comes to their behaviours, attitudes and interactions in the workplace?

Most organisations have some form of cultural agreement. It usually sits in the SoaP (Strategy on a Page, which I touched on in chapter 15) under values, behaviours or 'what we stand for' and lists words like integrity, trust, respect, teamwork and communication.

Sadly, many of these cultural agreements are just words on a page, and they hold very little meaning within the actual culture. They are corporatised words that really shouldn't have to be called out as they are the fundamental basics of being a decent human being. I mean, do we really have to call out trust and respect as behaviours we want in a workplace? Surely these should be a given!

These days, we are seeing organisations become more creative in this space and use language that their teams create and are connected to, including short statements rather than just a word. One of my favourite clients, SGUA and PIP, created its five statements depicting its culture:

1. We Own It and We Do It.

2. Think Big.

3. Together We Are Better.

4. We Are the Answer.

5. Be Curious.

SGUA and PIP included every employee in several sessions that started from a blank sheet to forming the statements they now live and breathe. Every initiative, every AGM, every reward and recognition and every communication links back to at least one of these values.

## Ask

How would you define your workplace culture? What are the values and behaviours that form your culture agreement, and do they really hold meaning? How psychologically safe does your team feel? What actions are required right now to improve the levels of environmental trust in your workplace?

Having an environment of trust helps the team to feel safe and connected. How your team feel when they are at work directly influences your performance and culture.

## *The 3Cs*

Creating these values and behaviours is a lot of fun and quite energising for everyone involved. It isn't hard to do. What is hard is the next steps, the 3Cs:

1. commitment

2. call-out

3. consequences.

It's not enough to just create and communicate. To really bring this to life there must be a wholehearted commitment (and buy-in) from everyone in the team. If we are serious about this, it becomes our identity and that means everyone who represents our company lives and breathes this. It is so much more than just emailing the statement around to everyone or putting it on the wall. It's the explanations and activities that help to make it relatable. It's leading by example and demonstrating how these values directly relate to what we deliver.

But understanding and commitment are still not enough. There must be a safe and agreed-upon call-out so that when these are not being lived or followed, people feel the trust in the environment to call it out and increase all levels of awareness. Our tone, words, body language and environment are all going to come into this call-out, so decide upfront how and when it is acceptable to call out so everyone is aligned before it happens.

We would hope that commitment and call-out should trigger emotional intelligence within us; however, the mind is pretty cheeky at times. It will always weigh up 'What do

I stand to gain by doing this?' vs 'What do I stand to lose by not doing this?' This is where consequences become a vital third step. To create and maintain an environment of trust aligned to our cultural agreement, there must be some kind of consequence for not living these values and behaviours. It doesn't matter how large or small the consequence is, there has to be one; otherwise, the trust in the environment and each other will deplete.

Simon Sinek tells the story that when he was working with the Marine Corps one of the team members fell asleep on their watch in the woods, resulting in him being let go. When Sinek questioned the harshness of the consequence, they explained that it wasn't falling asleep that resulted in the outcome; it was because when they questioned him about it, he denied it. When questioned again, he still denied it. It wasn't until they gave him irrefutable proof that he decided to take responsibility for his action. This did not align with the focus and cultural agreement that they had around trust. The Marine Corps wants its team members to take ownership when the action occurs, not when they are caught out. Their trust in this marine was diminished, and had there not been a consequence, the other marines would see that the leaders were all talk and not really delivering on the cultural agreement. The standards would slip, and the cultural agreement would become just words on a page.

I recently worked with a telco company that had an extremely impressive positive culture among its employees, and a fantastic culture agreement and purpose hanging on the wall. I could tell the minute I walked in that this was a fun place to work, and this was confirmed by employees' comments such as, 'This is the best place I've ever worked' and 'We have so much fun working here and we're the best in our industry'.

Between sessions, I had discussions with several of their leaders, who were struggling with difficult conversations relating to underperformance and unacceptable behaviour. They said these were definitely anomalies in their team and that the rest of the team were great. They also expressed how supportive the company is, but one person in particular was taking advantage of the company being so generous and supportive and was taking them for a bit of a ride.

On talking them through the approach to difficult conversations, it seemed that they were doing all the right things and having the right difficult conversations, but there was one rather large thing missing in their cultural agreement…the last area of the 3Cs: consequences. The expectations were communicated, there was a commitment from everyone (with follow-ups) and call-outs were happening in these difficult conversations, but there were no consequences.

One of the leaders talked about how, after the first conversation, the underperforming team member really turned around their attitude and was doing so much better, but then started to lapse again, bringing them back to where they started. I questioned the leader on what they did when they saw the individual lapsing. Unfortunately, the answer was 'nothing'. They had just hoped this individual would improve again. But they hadn't and now they were back at square one starting the process and difficult conversations again.

Oh dear, this is not what should be happening!

Two things had occurred here. Firstly, the cultural agreement of the team and company had been damaged because not addressing this behaviour had pretty much endorsed it and communicated to everyone that the cultural agreement was simply words on a page with no real commitment. Secondly, there was no consequence. So, regardless of whether or not this employee and all the others were aware of it, their subconscious mind was thinking, 'Do we really need to do it or worry about *this* if there is nothing to lose?'

What should have happened in this situation is that, the minute the leader noticed the first sign of a lapse, a conversation should have taken place. The area of concern should have been discussed using difficult conversation techniques and the consequences should have been made very clear. Should this behaviour have continued, there was no need to start right back at the beginning. They could have picked up where they left off with their last underperformance conversation, engaged their HR team and understood the process, but they would not have had to start fresh again. Poor behaviour should be enough to result in consequences. If this is not the case, you have a much bigger problem than this one person on your hands: you have a systemic cultural issue.

Not too long ago, I worked with an amazing organisation to help train and coach a group of senior leaders specifically on how to step up and interact with the executive leadership team. We prepped the team over several sessions, and they were ready to go, despite experiencing quite a few nerves when they were around the executives.

At the end of their first full day of stepping up and working with the executive team, the feedback was that they really under-delivered. The executive team had expected and wanted more and, overall, were disappointed. Naturally, this was upsetting to hear.

We reflected and dug deeper into the day's events from every angle. It seemed that the executives had already noticed early in the day that things weren't going well, but they hadn't done anything about it. They didn't call it out, reset expectations or create an environment of trust and permission to be nervous. They didn't allow the senior leaders to give it a go and not be absolutely perfect first go without judgement. The senior leaders' nerves got the better of them and while they stayed silent, the day progressed without any consequences. Their minds weighed up what they had to gain vs what they had to lose and given the loss was non-existent at the time and the gain was being blocked by nerves, they took the easy way out and became passengers rather than contributors and drivers. It was clear that both the senior leaders and the executive leaders had played a role in this underwhelming performance. There was work to be done with the executive leaders as well to get them applying the 3Cs more successfully, having difficult conversations and building an environment of trust, including psychological safety and an active cultural agreement.

## Ask

Are you delivering in all the 3Cs? What impact have the 3Cs had on the performance of your team? What will you do differently to ensure the 3Cs are evident in all areas of your team and organisation?

The mind will always look for the path of least resistance or the easy way. Asking someone or having someone commit is not enough, the weigh-up in their mind based on the value vs consequences overwrites the commitment.

# Individual trust

Trust goes deeper than just the environment. The people who make up the team and the culture and those people who fill the environment are also looking for trust in each other at an individual level.

There are so many things that contribute to our ability to trust someone. Some of these are hard to put into words: those deep, guttural instincts that hit us, or our intuition kicking in from our fight-or-flight response telling us to be careful or to be aware. Conversely, sometimes we meet people and — based on who they are, what they look like and their energy level — we decide instantly that we trust or distrust them, with no evidence to back up our thoughts.

With all these factors in play, there are six common dominant areas that we can break down to really understand where the trust and distrust lie. These are:

- honesty and transparency
- accountability and credibility
- empathy and vulnerability.

We group them together into three areas because some of them are quite similar and easily confused. It is not one or the other; they are separate areas, but it's easier to explain them side by side.

Knowing what is driving our levels of trust means we have an area to focus on or work within to increase the trust level. Without this understanding, we are stuck — with the overarching, broad outcome of trust or distrust being the end story.

As we step through these six areas, I want you to think of an individual you don't completely trust. Once you have read about an area, give yourself a rating out of 5 based on your level of trust in that area. You will notice that I said 'give *yourself* a rating'. The reason for this is that you are not rating them — you are rating your level of trust in them in that area. For example, how honest do you believe this person to be? A 5 is extremely honest and a 1 is no honesty at all. Do the same with transparency and the other four areas.

## *Honesty and transparency*

Honesty tends to be more emotionally driven than transparency. It comes with a process of sharing feelings, while transparency is more the process of sharing information. I can be transparent with you without letting you know how I really feel about it, whereas if I'm honest with you, you are more likely to hear not only the information but also how I feel about it (and sometimes you'll hear how I feel about it instead of the information itself). Honesty sounds like:

- 'Can I be honest?'
- 'Honestly...'
- 'To tell the truth...'

I worked at a company decades ago where the CEO liked to ban these statements. His concern was that, if you are saying this does that mean you are lying to me or being dishonest at other times? Obviously, this is not the case. We tend to use statements like these when we are communicating from our subconscious mind or about to share something that makes us feel a little vulnerable or nervous about how it will be received, so we preface it with the above statements to feel safer. So, when you hear someone start a sentence with any of these, know that what they are about to say is a deep feeling or thought for them. No, they are not lying to you every other time. But this time, listen very carefully because they are about to bare something from their subconscious mind.

Transparency sounds like:

- 'I'll tell you exactly what happened'
- 'Here is where we are at ... '
- 'I'll show you everything'.

This is information share: the opening up, but not necessarily the emotion or beliefs that I have attached to the situation. It's usually very factual and comes from our logical brain.

Rate the person you have in mind out of 5 separately for both transparency and honesty.

## Accountability and credibility

Accountability is when we take responsibility for actions. We deliver when required and there is a level of ownership in there. Anyone should be able to tell whether we are accountable or not. Did we do what we said we were going to do? It is how we interpret their level of quality and we tend to personally know them or know of them and their ability. There is a level of belief in the person who has credibility. Their reputation and our experience with them drive how credible we believe they are.

Accountability sounds like:

- 'I can do that for you'
- 'I will have it completed'
- 'I know I can count on them'.

Accountability is more about taking the steps and doing the action than knowing that this is the best person to deliver in this area. Someone can be accountable but doesn't need to come up with the answer or outcome themselves. If they get the answer or outcome, they have been accountable.

Credibility sounds like:

- 'They know what they are doing'
- 'I believe in them'
- 'I know they are the right person for this'.

There is connection and a form of relationship that seems deeper with credibility than with accountability. They are the expert in this space; they will deliver quality in what they do. There is a level of intelligence in whatever it is we find them credible in. While we can call or reference ourselves as being accountable, being called credible is usually a decision other people make about us.

Someone can be either or both accountable and/or credible, yet not be a very nice person as they go about it. They may be the best in the game, and they might always do what they say they will do, but they could still lack transparency or honesty in the process.

Rate the person you have in mind out of 5 separately for both accountability and credibility.

## Empathy and vulnerability

Empathy is when we focus on others, while vulnerability is when the focus is on us. With empathy, we care about their emotional state. We don't need to know what happened that led to this state. There is no room for judgement of whether they are feeling the right emotion or whether it is situational. We simply care about their emotions. When we are vulnerable, it's about how we feel. We are sharing our deepest thoughts and emotions. It's exposing ourselves and risking a feeling of loss of security or safety by other people knowing our feelings.

Empathy sounds like:

- actively listening
- 'It sounds like you are feeling...'
- 'How do we fix this or how can I support you through this?'

It's all about the emotion being felt, recognising what is the worst thing to hear when you are feeling this emotion and making sure we don't say that. It's ensuring we respond with the best thing we would want to hear if we were feeling this emotion.

Vulnerability sounds like:

- 'This makes me feel...'
- 'I am struggling...'
- 'I haven't told anyone...'

Empathy and vulnerability come from deep in our thoughts and open our potential fears of being judged.

**Moments of vulnerability talk to our subconscious minds and tend to trigger the other person's subconscious mind, feelings and emotions.**

Rate the person you have in mind out of 5 separately for both empathy and vulnerability.

• • •

What were your scores for each of the six areas? It's very normal to distrust someone even if they score high in one of these areas. If you found yourself scoring 1s in all areas, ensure that you are not in an emotional hijack and being driven by your emotional brain with little or no logical brain in play. At times, we may not be ready ourselves. Maybe we haven't owned it and faced our own emotions yet, in order to be ready to feel the emotion from the other person's point of view.

To increase our individual trust in someone else, we have got to want to increase the level of trust. It can't be forced upon us. There must come a time where we want to understand what is driving the distrust and have the drive to do something about it. We need to want to improve the relationship between us and the other person, especially if this is in the workplace. Unless we plan on leaving, we need to find a way to make it work. If we can identify where it is that the trust is lacking, we can then address it and create actions to improve it.

I once had someone in my team who was always accountable. They delivered every time. They were pretty much the most credible person in their field. Though they were transparent in every way and had the ability to empathise with others, they had never been vulnerable themselves and therefore didn't come across as completely honest. I found it really hard to trust them because I felt like they were always holding back.

Once I understood where my lack of trust in them was, we sat down and had a conversation, during which I voiced how much respect I had for this person in their accountability, transparency, credibility and empathy. About how I looked up to them in these areas and how they were truly amazing. I then shared that I struggled to completely trust them with my vulnerability and honesty because I felt like they weren't vulnerable or honest with me. It was a limitation in our relationship. The conversation itself became both honest and vulnerable and completely changed our relationship—though, as the saying goes, 'It didn't happen overnight, but it did happen'. Our relationship grew and my levels of individual trust in this person also grew.

Another example was a person I felt was being transparent, honest (maybe even too honest at times), caring, empathetic and vulnerable, but they just didn't quite deliver. The accountability wasn't too bad as they did deliver to a certain level in that area, but the credibility of what they delivered was extremely poor, which made it difficult for me to trust them. I initiated the difficult conversation with them and after a bit of defensive pushback, they owned a skill gap that they had previously hidden and denied within themselves, which we could then act on and further develop. The level of accountability and credibility increased, along with their skills. And, naturally, so did my level of trust in them.

## The only thing we have control of in this world is ourselves and the way we choose to react

I'm like a broken record in saying this — or maybe I'd be a millionaire if I got a dollar every time I said it — the only thing we have control of in this world is ourselves and the way we choose to react. No-one can make us feel an emotion. We choose how we feel based on our neural pathways, beliefs, values, memories and habits. We can't make anyone more trustworthy if we don't take ownership of the role we are playing in the situation. We are the ones who decide on the level of trust we have in others. If we don't want to improve the trust and relationship, or if we don't have the difficult conversation, that's our choice. If we want things to improve, we need to do something within our own control. Be emotionally intelligent. Understand the drivers creating the distrust and identify ways to improve them. We might be the only one struggling with this person in this area. It might not be them at all — it might be an embedded belief within us. Or it might totally be them, and we've tried everything we can to improve our relationship, but it didn't work. Either way, own the reality of the situation and move forward with the choices you made.

## Ask

What will it take for your team to become aligned and have trust? What is one thing you could do today to make a difference and provide the direction that is required to be high performing?

High performance is not something that is achieved simply through talent and ability. High performance is an agreement. An agreement of alignment, trust and communication between people. Without all three of these, high performance as a team will never be achieved.

# Chapter reflection

- Trust is made up of both environmental trust and individual trust.

- Environmental trust comes from a psychologically safe workplace and a cultural agreement that personally connects with the team.

- The 3Cs, commitment, call-out and consequences, are the foundations of a great culture that includes trust and connection to the identity of the team and workplace.

- Individual trust can be improved once we recognise and own what specific area the trust is lacking. We have got to want to improve the trust for this to happen.

- On reflection of trust, what is the current level of environmental trust in your workplace? How can you improve this trust and create connection to who you are as a team and workplace? What will you do to better understand your own levels of trust in the people around you?

# CONCLUSION: THE EMOTIONALLY INTELLIGENT WORKPLACE

Much like there not being an 'emotionally intelligent person', there isn't an emotionally intelligent workplace.

Sure, we can do everything we want to encourage, implement tools, provide training and embed EI into a workplace, but it will never actually be an emotionally intelligent workplace.

Why? Because we are human beings, and we will get things wrong at times. Our workplace won't always be perfect because the people in it aren't always perfect. This means there will be situations that aren't very emotionally intelligent. To call our workplace an emotionally intelligent workplace sets an expectation that we are always emotionally intelligent in every single situation, and this just isn't realistic. 'Always' is a big call when it comes to human beings.

So we must accept that we can have the best intentions, tools and people in place in the workplace, but we also need to have an understanding of how we will respond when things don't go to plan.

When we are serious about EI in our workplace, it becomes part of the agenda. Not just one agenda, but every agenda!

Over the decades, we have seen the 'customer' embedded in workplace strategies, operations and people. It became the limelight and the driver of customer-centric designs, customer-driven purpose, structures and initiatives. This is what is required to really embed EI in our workplaces.

The EI process, change intelligence, difficult conversations and high performance are daily occurrences for many workplaces. To roll out training without embedment is not going to be enough for it to be front of mind when these occur daily. We want people to be thinking about EI in everything they do. This happens with repetition. It doesn't just start from the top down; it starts at every level and flows in every direction simultaneously.

# Embedding EI in the workplace

To help you embed EI in your workplace, keep the following five tips in mind:

1. *Provide emotional intelligence training for every member of your workplace.* This can't be covered in a one- or two-hour session. This should be an ongoing program that involves some tough love aligned to your organisation. It should be a mixture of theory, case studies and actions to build knowledge, relatability and implementation of the learnings into

accountable situations. There should be resources that everyone can refer to in books, processes and coaches. Creating a specialty role or team for this would be incredible support for your organisation.

2. *Ensure that the EI process becomes a commonly discussed process in your workplace.* When referring to people, whether it is during change, conversations, performance or any area, use the common language of the EI process in part I to identify and communicate where the person is in relation to the process and to understand what it will take to get them to the next step. Reflect at all levels on how well each step of the process is being delivered individually and as teams, both internally and externally. Have an open communication forum to call out and discuss when steps in the process are missed.

3. *Remember that change intelligence is a part of every change-management plan.* Regardless of the size of the change, change intelligence should be a required step in the change plan, the same as research and testing are. The project team or people implementing the change shouldn't be signing off on the change until change intelligence has been reviewed and implemented. This includes a post-implementation review. A change-management model is not enough without the change intelligence piece.

4. *Never avoid difficult conversations—instead, embrace them with humanistic intent.* Each conversation is timely and is led by purpose and emotion with equal balance. The action and effectiveness of these conversations form part of the measure of leadership. The leaders across the

workplace have the right training and support to deliver these conversations with success regardless of whether they are managing up, down or sideways.

5. *Ensure teams are high performing with alignment, trust and strong communication.* Culture agreements are in place with the 3Cs and psychological safety are measured at least twice a year. The teams have clear direction, and every time they come together as a team, they have a permanent meeting agenda item that asks, 'How emotionally intelligent have we been since we last caught up?' They can provide examples of when, why, what, how and who along with learnings from each situation. These examples are easy to recall because they come from the self-reflection that each person does on a weekly (minimum) basis, asking themselves, 'What went well this week?', 'What didn't go so well?', 'What will I do to improve this for next week?' and finally, 'How emotionally intelligent have I been and, more importantly, what am I doing to improve this?'

● ● ●

I'm now handing the baton over to you. I've shared many tools, processes and guides in this book to build your EI, but reading a book is not enough: it's what you choose to do with this information that is the true commitment of your EI. What will you do? What is your first step to improving EI within yourself and your workplace?

Come and connect with me through my website (amyjacobson.com.au). I'd love to hear how you are owning it and what you are doing!

**It's time for you to Own It, take control and be unstoppable!**